الحقيقة على الباطل **truth over falsehood**

Are we there yet? Why not?

When you look through my eyes what do you see?

Sayyar Ismail Swift

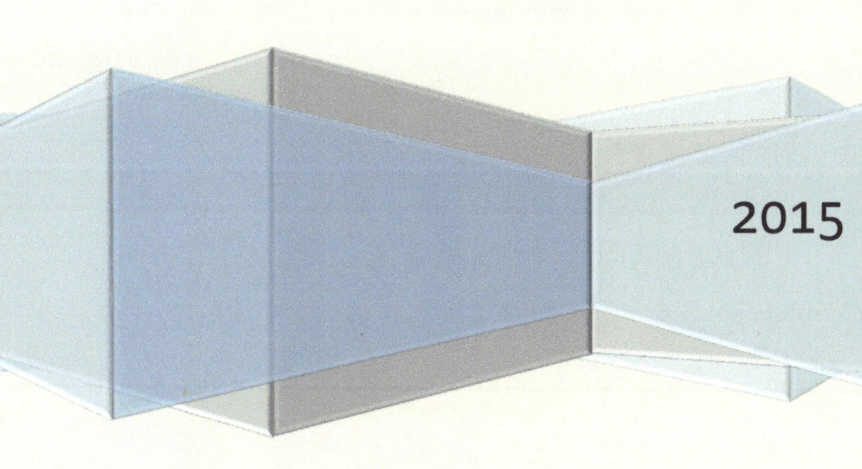

2015

Contents

Works Cited 4

Published in the Stanford Law and Policy Review (https://www.hrw.org/news/2009/06/19/race-drugs-and-law-enforcement-united-states). 4

Introduction 6

The equation of war 9

    Year-by-year Timeline of America's Major Wars (1776-2011) 9

    The effects of war on a society 17

Fundamental flaws and the true ideal behind the design 20

The King 24

Who is the king? 27

When was the republic high-jacked 31

Philosophical /political majority vs minority 36

Battle between the sexes 40

The hip/hop culture 47

Black woman/black man 56

One such recent conspiracy theory 60

Required Action 63

Works Cited

The Huffington Post by Brittany Wong
http://www.huffingtonpost.com/2014/12/02/divorce-rate

http://www.huffingtonpost.com/2014/11/25/divorce-rate-stats_n_6220124.html

Sayyar Isma'il Blog/books/ poetry (http://sayyarismail.weebly.com/blog-country-or-corporation, 2015.

http://www.washingtonsblog.com/2015/02/america-war-93-time-222-239-years-since-1776.html

http://2012books.lardbucket.org/books/culture-and-media/s12-02-the-relationship-between-telev.html

https://en.wikipedia.org/wiki/African-American_middle_class

http://www.pewresearch.org/fact-tank/2015/02/23/6-facts-about-black-americans-for-black-history-month/

http://www.fromthewilderness.com/free/pandora/blacks-targeted.html).

http://www.123rf.com/search.php?word=inner+city+poverty&start=100&t_word=&t_lang=en&imgtype=0&orisearch=inner%20city&searchopts=&itemsperpage=100

Published in the Stanford Law and Policy Review
(https://www.hrw.org/news/2009/06/19/race-drugs-and-law-enforcement-united-states).
(http://www.truth-out.org/opinion/item/16065-ronald-reagan-made-the-war-on-drugs-a-race-to-incarcerate).

Posted by Lena on October 30, 2013
http://www.theafrolounge.com/2013/10/30/conspiracy-theory-black-people-being-murdered-for-their-organs/.

http://melanoidnation.org/feds-raid-chicago-operation-linked-to-detroit-body-parts-business/.

(https://en.wikipedia.org/wiki/Tuskegee_syphilis_experiment.

http://www.enotes.com/homework-help/what-effects-war-society-400685

World Psychiatry 2006 Feb...
http://www.ncbi.nlm.nih.gov/pmc/articles/PMC1472271/citedby/.

https://en.wikipedia.org/wiki/Monarch

https://en.wikipedia.org/wiki/Economic_democracy*https://en.wikipedia.org/wiki/Divine_right_of_kings*

http://www.lexrex.com/enlightened/AmericanIdeal/aspects/demrep.html

http://www.britannica.com/event/Battle-of-New-Orleans-American-Civil-War-1862

http://www.thefiscaltimes.com/Articles/2011/04/12/Civil-War-at-150-Debt-Lessons-from-Lincoln

(https://www.youtube.com/watch?v=kuRTXRBB5Vo

http://www.vanityfair.com/news/2006/08/norad200608

Introduction

Are we there yet? No, then that only leaves the question as to why aren't we??? Today's capitalistic mindset of corporatized living and consumption has driven humanity in evolutionary ways of development, but has it been beneficial? Is mankind in the 21 century better off than his predecessor of 100, 200, 300 or 2000 years? That same question applies to the African & Black folks in America in likeness to recent colonialization. What about Pre-colonial times of Empires and there invading armies who occupied & usurped the wealth of foreign lands... Varying responses and answers I would bet depending upon who you asked and their particular backgrounds.

Neither far-fetched nor irrelevant in revisiting...for it supposedly knows the past which helps to shape the future...but has mankind lost his past? Somewhere along our journey we began to deviate from the end goal of arriving at a place of good for all...Our own absent mindedness and failure to understand has brought us to our knees in living. Our governments have made major shifts in deviating from the core objectives and principals behind the living, breathing document of the Constitution, which today seems to be in the ICU very bad hurt with major lacerations and amputations. History is the living model of trial and error that will always give us a glimpse back in time to consequences to similar path walked...so why is it that those same paths seem to be arrogantly decided upon still today? Have we really become that much less astute in brain power from technological dependency to the point where we blindly ignore the past, or is it by well thought out design and implementation to keep present course? Well, my answer is the latter...Yes many of us have forgotten the truth nature of laws that govern us while other could careless and therefore policy makers have run-amuck with decimating the integrity of our personal liberties and rights. Born into the world naked and free is the creator's intention; however man has taken upon himself to enslave his fellow man by laws by which he binds others to life-time servitude...Lies and doctrine history with political rhetoric that calls to the grouping and fragmenting of society. Man is very cunning in his deviance but seemingly dumb otherwise, always taken to some other past time distraction. We have to regain course, and take action socially, politically, & spiritually in cleaning up this huge mess of rubbish and deceitful confusion conveniently placed and propagated to further deviate the masses from the truth...

We know of the many conquest noted throughout history much of the libraries, in more modern claims to victory, where often the casualty of arrogance & deviance. The world long thriving in civizalations in Africa, the East of Asian, Indonesia and the Americas...today's history doesn't reflect most of those civilisations nor does their knowledge in common history books. Victims of racial pride and hidden from the general body, their stories are well-kept secrets which, require tireless efforts in seeking out there hidden locations.

However; archeological findings as well as studies carried out on locations, cities structures, art, pottery etc. seem to have been the only means by which these ghostly figures have been shared with the rest of us...But, today fossil records uncovered are depicting and piecing together a truer story than the story previously written. The earth in her grand tale, is divulging all of her secrets and along with a degradation of humanity in the current crisis has seemed to also awaken mankind to a heightened and more inquisitive state of consciousness. At his worst, tends to bring out his best so-to-speak...How remarkable it's been to me that painted lies disguised & high jacked have been the main source of guidance for humanity into the present day future. Many of which, were unchallenged or drowned out by distance from those who knew the truth. The western world primarily, and in her efforts of assuming hegemony over her pioneering Eastern civilization, has in her doctrine erased the history of a black captives in securing their fate in servitude; but has also to successive generations' been able to culturally bias the entire world through this materialized existence romanticised by a fantasy, & a façade of the epitome liberty, life, and fair pursuit of happiness...

So, let's look into ourselves a bit; past, present, and future and see just how we fair from one age to the next...there are reasons for everything and humanities present course can definitely be subjected to past misguidance, personally/and societal irresponsibility's which have led to uninformed decisions & rotted characteristics. Seemingly better when he is at is worst...Mankind; so how bad do things have to become before the trend begins to move back in the positive direction?

The equation of war

What has been the toll of war of the populace of American's in the past 6 decades? Around the same time as Kennedy's assassination, horrific images from Vietnam were streaming into people's living rooms during the nation's first televised war. With five camera crews on duty in the Saigon bureau, news crews captured vivid details of the war in progress. Although graphic images were rarely shown on network TV, several instances of violence reached the screen, including a CBS report in 1965 that showed Marines lighting the thatched roofs of the villages of Cam Ne with Zippo lighters and an NBC news report in 1968 that aired coverage of South Vietnamese General Nguyen Ngoc Loan executing a captive on a Saigon street. Further images, of children being burned, scarred by napalm, running naked & prisoners being tortured; fueled the antiwar sentiments of many Americans. In addition, to the devastation caused by the president's death and the Vietnam War, Americans were also feeling the pressure of the Cold War—the clash between the United States and the Soviet Union in the years following World War II. This pressure was especially great during periods of tension throughout the 1950s and 1960s. This is recent history...but what about America as a whole? Many of us, unless we sit down and do the research are ignorant to just how engulfed in War America has been. The typical person will probably respond with just the last 15yrs or so with the wars in Iraq and Afghanistan...Very few of us will ever come into the real details of America's involvement. Have a look at the following timeline:

Year-by-year Timeline of America's Major Wars (1776-2011)

- 1776 – American Revolutionary War, Chickamauga Wars, Second Cherokee War, Pennamite-Yankee War
- 1777 – American Revolutionary War, Chickamauga Wars, Second Cherokee War, Pennamite-Yankee War
- 1778 – American Revolutionary War, Chickamauga Wars, Pennamite-Yankee War

- 1779 – American Revolutionary War, Chickamauga Wars, Pennamite-Yankee War
- 1780 – American Revolutionary War, Chickamauga Wars, Pennamite-Yankee War
- 1781 – American Revolutionary War, Chickamauga Wars, Pennamite-Yankee War
- 1782 – American Revolutionary War, Chickamauga Wars, Pennamite-Yankee War
- 1783 – American Revolutionary War, Chickamauga Wars, Pennamite-Yankee War
- 1784 – Chickamauga Wars, Pennamite-Yankee War, Oconee War
- 1785 – Chickamauga Wars, Northwest Indian War
- 1786 – Chickamauga Wars, Northwest Indian War
- 1787 – Chickamauga Wars, Northwest Indian War
- 1788 – Chickamauga Wars, Northwest Indian War
- 1789 – Chickamauga Wars, Northwest Indian War
- 1790 – Chickamauga Wars, Northwest Indian War
- 1791 – Chickamauga Wars, Northwest Indian War
- 1792 – Chickamauga Wars, Northwest Indian War
- 1793 – Chickamauga Wars, Northwest Indian War
- 1794 – Chickamauga Wars, Northwest Indian War
- 1795 – Northwest Indian War
- **1796 – No major war…1797 – No major war**
- 1798 – Quasi-War.1799 – Quasi-War…1800 – Quasi-War
- 1801 – First Barbary War…1802 – First Barbary War…1803 – First Barbary War (the Muslim Berber peoples of North Africa)
- 1804 – First Barbary War…1805 – First Barbary War
- 1806 – Sabine Expedition
- **1807 – No major war….1808 – No major war…1809 – No major war**
- 1810 – U.S. occupies Spanish-held West Florida
- 1811 – Tecumseh's War
- 1812 – War of 1812, Tecumseh's War, Seminole Wars, U.S. occupies Spanish-held Amelia Island and other parts of East Florida
- 1813 – War of 1812, Tecumseh's War, Peoria War, Creek War, U.S. expands its territory in West Florida
- 1814 – War of 1812, Creek War, U.S. expands its territory in Florida, Anti-piracy war
- 1815 – War of 1812, Second Barbary War, Anti-piracy war

- 1816 – First Seminole War, Anti-piracy war
- 1817 – First Seminole War, Anti-piracy war
- 1818 – First Seminole War, Anti-piracy war
- 1819 – Yellowstone Expedition, Anti-piracy war
- 1820 – Yellowstone Expedition, Anti-piracy war
- 1821 – Anti-piracy war (see note above)…1822 – Anti-piracy war (see note above)
- 1823 – Anti-piracy war, Arikara War…1824 – Anti-piracy war
- 1825 – Yellowstone Expedition, Anti-piracy war
- **1826 – No major war**
- 1827 – Winnebago War
- **1828 – No major war…1829 – No major war…1830 – No major war**
- 1831 – Sac and Fox Indian War
- 1832 – Black Hawk War
- 1833 – Cherokee Indian War
- 1834 – Cherokee Indian War, Pawnee Indian Territory Campaign
- 1835 – Cherokee Indian War, Seminole Wars, Second Creek War
- 1836 – Cherokee Indian War, Seminole Wars, Second Creek War, Missouri-Iowa Border War
- 1837 – Cherokee Indian War, Seminole Wars, Second Creek War, Osage Indian War, Buckshot War
- 1838 – Cherokee Indian War, Seminole Wars, Buckshot War, Heatherly Indian War
- 1839 – Cherokee Indian War, Seminole Wars
- 1840 – Seminole Wars, U.S. naval forces invade Fiji Islands
- 1841 – Seminole Wars, U.S. naval forces invade McKean Island, Gilbert Islands, and Samoa
- 1842 – Seminole Wars
- 1843 – U.S. forces clash with Chinese, U.S. troops invade African coast
- 1844 – Texas-Indian Wars…1845 – Texas-Indian Wars
- 1846 – Mexican-American War, Texas-Indian Wars
- 1847 – Mexican-American War, Texas-Indian Wars
- 1848 – Mexican-American War, Texas-Indian Wars, Cayuse War
- 1849 – Texas-Indian Wars, Cayuse War, Southwest Indian Wars, Navajo Wars, Skirmish between 1st Cavalry and Indians
- 1850 – Texas-Indian Wars, Cayuse War, Southwest Indian Wars, Navajo Wars, Yuma War, California Indian Wars, Pitt River Expedition

- 1851 – Texas-Indian Wars, Cayuse War, Southwest Indian Wars, Navajo Wars, Apache Wars, Yuma War, Utah Indian Wars, California Indian Wars
- 1852 – Texas-Indian Wars, Cayuse War, Southwest Indian Wars, Navajo Wars, Yuma War, Utah Indian Wars, California Indian Wars
- 1853 – Texas-Indian Wars, Cayuse War, Southwest Indian Wars, Navajo Wars, Yuma War, Utah Indian Wars, Walker War, California Indian Wars
- 1854 – Texas-Indian Wars, Cayuse War, Southwest Indian Wars, Navajo Wars, Apache Wars, California Indian Wars, Skirmish between 1st Cavalry and Indians
- 1855 – Seminole Wars, Texas-Indian Wars, Cayuse War, Southwest Indian Wars, Navajo Wars, Apache Wars, California Indian Wars, Yakima War, Winnas Expedition, Klickitat War, Puget Sound War, Rogue River Wars, U.S. forces invade Fiji Islands and Uruguay
- 1856 – Seminole Wars, Texas-Indian Wars, Southwest Indian Wars, Navajo Wars, California Indian Wars, Puget Sound War, Rogue River Wars, Tintic War
- 1857 – Seminole Wars, Texas-Indian Wars, Southwest Indian Wars, Navajo Wars, California Indian Wars, Utah War, Conflict in Nicaragua
- 1858 – Seminole Wars, Texas-Indian Wars, Southwest Indian Wars, Navajo Wars, Mohave War, California Indian Wars, Spokane-Coeur d'Alene-Paloos War, Utah War, U.S. forces invade Fiji Islands and Uruguay
- 1859 Texas-Indian Wars, Southwest Indian Wars, Navajo Wars, California Indian Wars, Pecos Expedition, Antelope Hills Expedition, Bear River Expedition, John Brown's raid, U.S. forces launch attack against Paraguay, U.S. forces invade Mexico
- 1860 – Texas-Indian Wars, Southwest Indian Wars, Navajo Wars, Apache Wars, California Indian Wars, Paiute War, Kiowa-Comanche War
- 1861 – American Civil War, Texas-Indian Wars, Southwest Indian Wars, Navajo Wars, Apache Wars, California Indian Wars, Cheyenne Campaign
- 1862 – American Civil War, Texas-Indian Wars, Southwest Indian Wars, Navajo Wars, Apache Wars, California Indian Wars, Cheyenne Campaign, Dakota War of 1862,
- 1863 – American Civil War, Texas-Indian Wars, Southwest Indian Wars, Navajo Wars, Apache Wars, California Indian Wars, Cheyenne Campaign, Colorado War, Goshute War
- 1864 – American Civil War, Texas-Indian Wars, Navajo Wars, Apache Wars, California Indian Wars, Cheyenne Campaign, Colorado War, Snake War

- 1865 – American Civil War, Texas-Indian Wars, Navajo Wars, Apache Wars, California Indian Wars, Colorado War, Snake War, Utah's Black Hawk War
- 1866 – Texas-Indian Wars, Navajo Wars, Apache Wars, California Indian Wars, Skirmish between 1st Cavalry and Indians, Snake War, Utah's Black Hawk War, Red Cloud's War, Franklin County War, U.S. invades Mexico, Conflict with China
- 1867 – Texas-Indian Wars, Long Walk of the Navajo, Apache Wars, Skirmish between 1st Cavalry and Indians, Snake War, Utah's Black Hawk War, Red Cloud's War, Comanche Wars, Franklin County War, U.S. troops occupy Nicaragua and attack Taiwan
- 1868 – Texas-Indian Wars, Long Walk of the Navajo, Apache Wars, Skirmish between 1st Cavalry and Indians, Snake War, Utah's Black Hawk War, Red Cloud's War, Comanche Wars, Battle of Wichita River, Franklin County War
- 1869 – Texas-Indian Wars, Apache Wars, Skirmish between 1st Cavalry and Indians, Utah's Black Hawk War, Comanche Wars, Franklin County War
- 1870 – Texas-Indian Wars, Apache Wars, Skirmish between 1st Cavalry and Indians, Utah's Black Hawk War, Comanche Wars, Franklin County War
- 1871 – Texas-Indian Wars, Apache Wars, Skirmish between 1st Cavalry and Indians, Utah's Black Hawk War, Comanche Wars, Franklin County War, Kingsley Cave Massacre, U.S. forces invade Korea
- 1872 – Texas-Indian Wars, Apache Wars, Utah's Black Hawk War, Comanche Wars, Modoc War, Franklin County War
- 1873 – Texas-Indian Wars, Comanche Wars, Modoc War, Apache Wars, Cypress Hills Massacre, U.S. forces invade Mexico
- 1874 – Texas-Indian Wars, Comanche Wars, Red River War, Mason County War, U.S. forces invade Mexico
- 1875 – Conflict in Mexico, Texas-Indian Wars, Comanche Wars, Eastern Nevada, Mason County War, Colfax County War, U.S. forces invade Mexico
- 1876 – Texas-Indian Wars, Black Hills War, Mason County War, U.S. forces invade Mexico
- 1877 – Texas-Indian Wars, Skirmish between 1st Cavalry and Indians, Black Hills War, Nez Perce War, Mason County War, Lincoln County War, San Elizario Salt War, U.S. forces invade Mexico

- 1878 – Paiute Indian conflict, Bannock War, Cheyenne War, Lincoln County War, U.S. forces invade Mexico
- 1879 – Cheyenne War, Sheepeater Indian War, White River War, U.S. forces invade Mexico
- 1880 – U.S. forces invade Mexico
- 1881 – U.S. forces invade Mexico
- 1882 – U.S. forces invade Mexico
- 1883 – U.S. forces invade Mexico
- 1884 – U.S. forces invade Mexico
- 1885 – Apache Wars, Eastern Nevada Expedition, U.S. forces invade Mexico
- 1886 – Apache Wars, Pleasant Valley War, U.S. forces invade Mexico
- 1887 – U.S. forces invade Mexico
- 1888 – U.S. show of force against Haiti, U.S. forces invade Mexico
- 1889 – U.S. forces invade Mexico
- 1890 – Sioux Indian War, Skirmish between 1st Cavalry and Indians, Ghost Dance War, Wounded Knee, U.S. forces invade Mexico
- 1891 – Sioux Indian War, Ghost Dance War, U.S. forces invade Mexico
- 1892 – Johnson County War, U.S. forces invade Mexico
- 1893 – U.S. forces invade Mexico and Hawaii
- 1894 – U.S. forces invade Mexico
- 1895 – U.S. forces invade Mexico, Bannock Indian Disturbances
- 1896 – U.S. forces invade Mexico
- **1897 – No major war**
- 1898 – Spanish-American War, Battle of Leech Lake, Chippewa Indian Disturbances
- 1899 – Philippine-American War, Banana Wars
- 1900 – Philippine-American War, Banana Wars
- 1901 – Philippine-American War, Banana Wars
- 1902 – Philippine-American War, Banana Wars
- 1903 – Philippine-American War, Banana Wars
- 1904 – Philippine-American War, Banana Wars
- 1905 – Philippine-American War, Banana Wars
- 1906 – Philippine-American War, Banana Wars
- 1907 – Philippine-American War, Banana Wars
- 1908 – Philippine-American War, Banana Wars
- 1909 – Philippine-American War, Banana Wars
- 1910 – Philippine-American War, Banana Wars

- 1911 – Philippine-American War, Banana Wars
- 1912 – Philippine-American War, Banana Wars
- 1913 – Philippine-American War, Banana Wars, New Mexico Navajo War
- 1914 – Banana Wars, U.S. invades Mexico
- 1915 – Banana Wars, U.S. invades Mexico, Colorado Paiute War
- 1916 – Banana Wars, U.S. invades Mexico
- 1917 – Banana Wars, World War I, U.S. invades Mexico
- 1918 – Banana Wars, World War I, U.S invades Mexico
- 1919 – Banana Wars, U.S. invades Mexico
- 1920 – Banana Wars
- 1921 – Banana Wars
- 1922 – Banana Wars
- 1923 – Banana Wars, Posey War
- 1924 – Banana Wars
- 1925 – Banana Wars
- 1926 – Banana Wars
- 1927 – Banana Wars
- 1928 – Banana Wars
- 1930 – Banana Wars
- 1931 – Banana Wars
- 1932 – Banana Wars
- 1933 – Banana Wars
- 1934 – Banana Wars…. **1935 – No major war… 1936 – No major war…1937 – No major war…1938 – No major war…1939 – No major war…1940 – No major war**
- 1941 – World War II…1942 – World War II…1943 – Wold War II…1944 – World War II…1945 – World War II
- 1946 – Cold War (U.S. occupies the Philippines and South Korea)
- 1947 – Cold War (U.S. occupies South Korea, U.S. forces land in Greece to fight Communists)
- 1948 – Cold War (U.S. forces aid Chinese Nationalist Party against Communists)
- 1949 – Cold War (U.S. forces aid Chinese Nationalist Party against Communists)
- 1950 – Korean War, Jayuga Uprising
- 1951 – Korean War…1952 – Korean War…1953 – Korean War
- 1954 – Covert War in Guatemala

- 1955 – Vietnam War…1956 – Vietnam War…1957 – Vietnam War…1958 – Vietnam War…1959 – Vietnam War, Conflict in Haiti…1960 – Vietam War…1961 – Vietnam War
- 1962 – Vietnam War, Cold War (Cuban Missile Crisis; U.S. marines fight Communists in Thailand)
- 1963 – Vietnam War…1964 – Vietnam War…1965 – Vietnam War, U.S. occupation of Dominican Republic…1966 – Vietnam War, U.S. occupation of Dominican Republic…1967 – Vietnam War…1968 – Vietnam War…1969 – Vietnam War
- 1970 – Vietnam War…1971 – Vietnam War…1972 – Vietnam War…1973 – Vietnam War, U.S. aids Israel in *Yom Kippur War*
- 1974 – Vietnam War…1975 – Vietnam War…
- **1976 – No major war…1977 – No major war…1978 – No major war**
- 1979 – Cold War (CIA proxy war in Afghanistan)…1980 – Cold War (CIA proxy war in Afghanistan)
- 1981 – Cold War (CIA proxy war in Afghanistan and Nicaragua), First Gulf of Sidra Incident
- 1982 – Cold War (CIA proxy war in Afghanistan and Nicaragua), Conflict in Lebanon
- 1983 – Cold War (Invasion of Grenada, CIA proxy war in Afghanistan and Nicaragua), Conflict in Lebanon
- 1984 – Cold War (CIA proxy war in Afghanistan and Nicaragua), Conflict in Persian Gulf
- 1985 – Cold War (CIA proxy war in Afghanistan and Nicaragua)
- 1986 – Cold War (CIA proxy war in Afghanistan and Nicaragua)
- 1987 – Conflict in Persian Gulf
- 1988 – Conflict in Persian Gulf, U.S. occupation of Panama
- 1989 – Second Gulf of Sidra Incident, U.S. occupation of Panama, Conflict in Philippines
- 1990 – First Gulf War, U.S. occupation of Panama
- 1991 – First Gulf War…1992 – Conflict in Iraq…1993 – Conflict in Iraq
- 1994 – Conflict in Iraq, U.S. invades Haiti
- 1995 – Conflict in Iraq, U.S. invades Haiti, NATO bombing of Bosnia and Herzegovina
- 1996 – Conflict in Iraq
- **1997 – No major war**
- 1998 – Bombing of Iraq, Missile strikes against Afghanistan and Sudan
- 1999 – Kosovo War

- 2000 – No major war
- 2001 – War on Terror in Afghanistan
- 2002 – War on Terror in Afghanistan and Yemen
- 2003 – War on Terror in Afghanistan, and Iraq
- 2004 – War on Terror in Afghanistan, Iraq, Pakistan, and Yemen
- 2005 – War on Terror in Afghanistan, Iraq, Pakistan, and Yemen
- 2006 – War on Terror in Afghanistan, Iraq, Pakistan, and Yemen
- 2007 – War on Terror in Afghanistan, Iraq, Pakistan, Somalia, and Yemen
- 2008 – War on Terror in Afghanistan, Iraq, Pakistan, and Yemen
- 2009 – War on Terror in Afghanistan, Iraq, Pakistan, and Yemen
- 2010 – War on Terror in Afghanistan, Iraq, Pakistan, and Yemen
- 2011 – War on Terror in Afghanistan, Iraq, Pakistan, Somalia, and Yemen; Conflict in Libya (Libyan Civil War)

In most of these wars, the U.S. was on the offense; some of the wars were defensive but the bulk was all offensive. Not to mention the exclusions of covert CIA operations and other acts which could be considered war…

Let's update what's happened since 2011:

1. 2012 – War on Terror in Afghanistan, Iraq, Somalia, Syria and Yemen
2. 2013 – War on Terror in Afghanistan, Iraq, Somalia, Syria and Yemen
3. 2014 – War on Terror in Afghanistan, Iraq, Somalia, Syria and Yemen; Civil War in Ukraine
4. 2015 – War on Terror in Somalia, Somalia, Syria and Yemen; Civil War in Ukraine

Adding 4 more years of war; that means that for 222 out of 239 years – or 93% of the time – America has been at war…
(http://www.washingtonsblog.com/2015/02/america-war-93-time-222-239-years-since-1776.html).

The effects of war on a society

Let's see, the cold-war resulted in the expansion & renewed emphasis placed on science and mathematics for technological advancements in order to compete with the Soviet Union. The space race is one such case in point…America became aware of the threats also of the nuclear arms race, expanded its industrialization. With the expansions many people obtained more material wealth, but the environment increased in pollution and mineral resources depleted. War can have many different impacts on societies. It depends very much on what the society is like before the war, what the war is about, how popular the war is, whether that particular country wins or loses the war, and many other variables. WWII had a positive impact on America because it drove the USA economy helping it out of the Great Depression. Solidarity and patriotism were also increased as the reasons beyond the war were seen and understood to be for the greater good; coupled with the economic boost the spirits of the people were very high. All of the seemingly good and new solidarity of the country also helped the black-folks of the country with civil-rights issues...But war should never be the electric shocks that jump start the economy again in the production of war materials. Human causalities are priceless in comparison, even just one life...

Among the consequences of war, the impact on the mental health of the civilian population is one of the most significant. Studies of the general population show a definite increase in the incidence and prevalence of mental disorders. Daily media bombardment of images beamed back showcasing the realities of war to the civilian population raises subconscious fear, and many times cements within the psyche the targeted outcomes of such propaganda. Really, when you think about it, why is it necessary to project these images to a civilian population other than to try and valid your case for war, and or political ideology in gaining support. War has a catastrophic effect on the health and well-being of nations. Studies have shown that conflict situations cause more mortality and disability than any major disease. War destroys communities and families and often disrupts the development of the social and economic fabric of nations. The effects of war include long-term physical and psychological harm to children and adults, as well as reduction in material and human capital. Death as a result of wars is simply the "tip of the iceberg" and oblivious consequence to war itself, but other consequences, besides death, are not well documented however; some after effects include endemic poverty, malnutrition, disability, economic/ social decline and psychosocial illness, to mention only a few.

But what about countries like America who are isolated from the rest of the world geographically? Besides the wars that helped establish America as a country, most of her wars have been fought on foreign soil. Even in wars where she has been declared the loser, the civilian population is spared from the devastating destruction of war and has only the shame of a boastful pride in returning home with a long face. Sure, economical vices may be incurred but the overall infrastructure remains to carry forward. Is there a psychological kickback on the population from war? Well, the biggest most severe is definitely the economy...and unlike the era of WWII where she was coming out of here depression, America's indebtedness as since folded onto itself many times over with yet an ever increasing military budget. Her budget today for military spending is more than ALL other nations combined...!!! That's crazy! Military spending is the reason why educational funds, school closing, repairs for infrastructure, government assets being sold (which actually belong to the citizens), social programs, health care, Social security, 401k & pensions are all cut short or done away with completely. The economic woes are by far the most important thing to most Americans that it usually over-shadows the opinions of politics other than for reasons of jobs i.e. money...foreign policy isn't something that concerns most people, although that percentage maybe increasing today, its remained ignored for many decades by most people in their lifetimes.

So, classism is redefining its boundaries as the upper-middle class gets swallowed back down into the bucket of crabs it work so hard to escape from. Exacerbated by other under-pinning differences; the situation is opposite of patriotically or solidifying national unity and up-swings in the economy that would be in the least bit beneficial. But, short-lived few at a time opportunities ripple out among the people, while things worsen. Unfortunately, it's the fate that America has sealed for herself having indulged in some degree 93% of the time she has been a country. I can't help but mention the contrast to the violence she partakes in foreign lands and the increased acts of violence within...not only the frequency, but the magnitude of each. It's clear that most people have become desensitised to the violent acts and images, beyond the initial shock of unsuspected perpetrators or newly seen events not before witnessed. Then a sort of melancholy descends and everything is just absorbed like the rain is absorbed into a dry earth...

Fundamental flaws and the true ideal behind the design

"Pure democracy cannot subsist long nor be carried far into the departments of state; it is very subject to caprice and the madness of popular rage."

— John Witherspoon (1722-1794) Educator, Economist, Minister, Writer & Founding Father

"The known propensity of a democracy is to licentiousness which the ambitious call, and ignorant believe to be liberty."

— Fisher Ames (1758-1808) Founding Father and framer of the First Amendment to the Constitution

Just after the completion and signing of the Constitution, in reply to a woman's inquiry as to the type of government the Founders had created, **Benjamin Franklin** *said,* "**A Republic, if you can keep it**."

What an interesting statement...Why do you suppose he said this? **A Republic** is representative government ruled by law (**the United States Constitution**). **A Democracy** is government ruled by the majority (*mob rule*). A Republic recognizes the unalienable rights of individuals while Democracies are only concerned with group wants or needs for the good of the public or in other words social justice.

- Lawmaking is a slow, deliberate process in our Constitutional **Republic** requiring approval from the three branches of government, the Legislative, Executive, and Judicial branches for checks and balance. Lawmaking in **Democracy** occurs rapidly requiring approval from the majority by polls and/or voter referendums, which in turn is mob rule 50% plus 1 vote takes away anything from the minority.

- Here is one example; if 51% of the people don't pay taxes they can vote a tax increase on the 49% that do, which is mob rule

Now, here's an interesting point, something that you may have not considered: In order for a democracy *to maintain their power, these candidates must adopt an ever-increasing tax and spend policy to satisfy the ever-increasing desires of the majority. As taxes increase, incentive to produce decreases, causing many of the once productive to drop out and join the non-productive. When there are no longer enough producers to fund the legitimate functions of government and the socialist programs, the democracy will collapse, <u>always to be followed by a Dictatorship.</u> This is the cusp the America finds herself today...what else explains the heightened police state of America, and all of their outrageous actions resulting in so many deaths of black citizens? Not to mention the implementation of Jade helm 15 and other pre-martial law practices taking place around the country reading those to impose it.*

<u>*Article IV Section 4*</u>, of the Constitution "*The United States shall guarantee to every State in this Union a Republican Form of government, and shall protect each of them against Invasion*", the word Democracy is not mentioned in the Constitution at all...How many knew that? So, tell me again what you think you're fighting to uphold or what you try to carbon copy upon other people around the world who know better...

Have a look at some of the quotes made by those who constructed the Constitution and otherwise...

- "Hence it is that democracies have ever been spectacles of turbulence and contention; have ever been found incompatible with personal security or the rights of property; and in general have been as short in their lives as they have been violent in their deaths... A republic, by which I mean a government in which a scheme of representation takes place, opens a different prospect and promises the cure for which we are seeking." **James Madison, Federalist Papers No. 10 (1787).**

- "Democracy is two wolves and a lamb voting on what to have for lunch. Liberty is a well-armed lamb contesting the vote!" **Ben Franklin**

- "A democracy is nothing more than mob rule, where fifty-one percent of the people may take away the rights of the other forty-nine." **Thomas Jefferson**

- "Remember, democracy never lasts long. It soon wastes, exhausts, and murders itself. There never was a democracy yet that did not commit suicide." **John Adams**

- "But government in which the majority rule in all cases cannot be based on justice, even as far as men understand it." **Henry David Thoreau**

"We are a Republic. Real Liberty is never found in despotism or in the extremes of Democracy."
— Alexander Hamilton (1755-1804) Lawyer, Secretary of the Treasury & Secretary of State

"A simple democracy is the devil's own government."
— Benjamin Rush (1745-1813) Founding Father & signer of the Declaration of Independence

"Let the American youth never forget that they possess a noble inheritance, bought by the toils and sufferings and blood of their ancestors, and capable, if wisely improved and faithfully guarded, of transmitting to the latest posterity all the substantial blessings of life, the peaceful enjoyment of liberty, property, religion, and independence. The structure has been erected by architects of consummate skill and fidelity; its foundations are solid, its compartments are beautiful as well as useful, its arrangements are full of wisdom and order, and its defenses are impregnable from without. It has been reared for immortality, if the work of men may justly aspire to such a title. It may nevertheless perish in an hour by the folly, or corruption, or negligence of its only keepers, the People. Republics are created by the virtue, public spirit, and intelligence of the citizens. They fall when the wise are banished from the public councils because they dare to be honest, and the profligate are rewarded because they flatter the people in order to betray them."

— Joseph Story (1779-1845) Lawyer, Supreme Court Justice & influential commentators on the U.S. Constitution

Whether or not it excluded you in the past...it needs to be learned and enforced today. Ignorant and taught otherwise, while others really don't even care...this document is the umbrella that explains the land of USA. It's very irresponsible to live without participating in the justice of yourself and all people. This laziness and carelessness of the people is exactly the way the few that control everything see you, and therefore you're expendable...If you don't care why should they? Furthermore, why should they care about your rights to exist when they see you as so much less...just here using up resources as they would put it...the following quote(s) made long ago gives amazing accuracy to the collective in America today...

"Democracy will soon degenerate into an anarchy; such an anarchy that every man will do what is right in his own eyes and no man's life or property or reputation or liberty will be secure, and every one of these will soon mould itself into a system of subordination of all the moral virtues and intellectual abilities, all the powers of wealth, beauty, wit, and science, to the wanton pleasures, the capricious will, and the execrable [abominable] cruelty of one or a very few."

— John Adams (1797-1801) Second President of the United States and Patriot

"A democracy is a volcano, which conceals the fiery materials of its own destruction. These will produce an eruption, and carry desolation in their way."

— Fisher Ames (1758-1808) Founding Father and framer of the First Amendment to the Constitution...

The King

Now reacquainted with the premise of fundamental flaws of democracy and what the founding fathers of the USA constitution and other drafters/advisors to it had to say; we should hopefully be able to intelligently see why we haven't arrived yet to a tranquil just means of existence...

Through documented speech of the Prophet Muhammad s.a.w. he says only 4 people have ever ruled the entire world...Two with submission to the creator and establishing rule on divine decree; and the latter two on the whims of their own divinity, pride, and arrogances...

1. Dhul-Qarnine (The king who traveled the entire known world in his time; his story is also known amongst the Jews, but I don't know about the Christians) He Established and ruled by divine law...
2. King/Prophet Sulaiman a.s. (Solomon), heir to King/Prophet Dawud a.s (David) who fought many wars in establishing divine rule over the tribes who had taken to idolatry...
3. Nimrod (Babylon and the tower of Babylon) ruled by his own whims calling himself a "god"...
4. King Bukhtanasar (Nebbacanser in English) In 587 BC *Bukhtanassar*, the king of Babylon, invaded Jerusalem, seized everything and demolished the structure of *Al-Aqsaa* mosque (called the dome of the rock today). He kept as captives all those who were not killed and took them to Babylon enslaving them for 70yrs.

Traveling now back in time to the age of Emperors, monarch, sovereign, sultan, czar, khan, caliph, or Caesar...history has always displayed governance from the leadership of an appointed leader over the people. Royalty and appointment to rule has come about by various types of assessments and or qualifications of which, one of the strongest claims is divine right. Lineage is then a close runner-up after having established the "divine right" to ruler-ship where then lineage would guarantee succession...this political/religious doctrine asserts that a "person" has the right to earthly authority...this right of authority is derived directly from the will of God, as those who would seek earthly authority by this means would say or think...

So, is this a valid decree? Of course it is...The famous account of God/the creator of everything appointing a king in recent recorded history would be that of Saul (the English name) Talut (Arabic) under the prophet hood of Samuel a.s. to Bani Israel (children of Israel) told in the Torah...his appointment was succeeded after his death by David (Dawud a.s) who was also a prophet, and then succeeded by his son Solomon (Sulaiman a.s.) also a prophet...These kings ruled by divine appointment and validate either by the prophet among them or in case of Dawud a.s. & Sulaiman a.s. they were prophets themselves. The last known case of divine rule was not the appointment of Kingship, but the re-establishment of divine law with Prophet Muhammad s.a.w. who revealed an abrogated law to last until the end of time. After his death s.a.w.; he was succeed by the Caliph. The Caliph was to rule by divine law, based on the prophetic model which was the validation of prior kings' mention by divine will. Now, that brings us to the premise of the book and the ruler-ship or governances of people... _Divine appointment requires ruler-ship based on divine law_, not man's law and thereby that statement alone brings understanding to the differences that we may see today within the remaining Monarchies. God's will requires his law, which has been brought by the prophets abrogated in succession until the last. There is absolutely no excuse if ruler-ship is based on something else. Without turning this into a religiously biased debate, I know that some readers would be inclined to comment on the validity of the previous statements, and the concurrence of such matters would probably boil down to faith/belief. But all 3 of the major religions confirm these statements and appointments and the respectful laws as beginning evidence, so I will continue on with my point...

Other kings have followed the justified divinely appointed kings, but their appointments weren't made by God's will in the sense that they didn't establish God's law in rule. Again some readers may argue the point again here and say that the Christian kings of Europe and the pope validate the claim to established divine law...I would rebut the claim with the denial of the last prophet Muhammad s.a.w. and the justly abrogated law of the Qur'an wasn't followed and thereby defeats any claim to established divine law in the land. Additionally, the Torah, besides being lost, isn't followed to the letter; nor is the Gospel of Esa ibn Mariam a.s...Lastly, I would then state, all of the evidence that has come by way of non-Islamic evidences (which bring the truth) that shatter those doctrines completely as to what they were made into being i.e. the mixture of paganism an adaptation of Emperor Constantine. In other cases it's the ideals of kings in the context of the Egyptians, who made themselves gods... Those adaptations have been carried over ever since; and thus no real claim can be made towards divine law governances by Europe.

Recent history saw the end to the Caliphate with the Ottoman Empire in the 1920's thus bringing divine rule to another holt; and all of the established Monarchies of Europe and even the ones in the Middle-East that carry on to present were NOT established by divine will! Thus there validity is based solely on political merit an appointment... Instead, they have always come in from the acquisition of power. Having control and intimate knowledge of those they commanded, military generals were often known for the coups they brought about in seizing political power. The rightly elected President Muhammad Morsey in Egypt was knocked down by his appointed general back by the west just recently during civil unrest and protest from the previous dictator Mubarak...Then their successions would be fought over by siblings also known to kill for power, and or other outsiders all trying to ascend to royalty. These later kingdoms turned tyrannical subjugation sought to administer complete dominance over their subjects and thus rule with absolute power. The king is thus not subject to the will of his people, the aristocracy, or any other estate of the realm, including (in the view of some, especially in Protestant countries or during the reign of Henry VIII of England) the Catholic Church. According to this doctrine, only God can judge an unjust king. The doctrine implies that any attempt to depose the king or to restrict his powers runs contrary to the will of God and may constitute a sacrilegious act and this is the adapted "divine rule" most carry out until this day. Although most of them have adopted this idea of democracy around them with electorate prime-ministers and other delegates to governing...The European model is in fact modeled on the caliphate model with the pope being the priestly figure to validate divine rule; but this premise in my opinion lacks the validity of a prophet to justify the claim. The authority of the church made by interpretation of Roman law; while Middle-eastern Monarchs are said to claim lineage back the Prophet Muhammad s.a.w. thus stacking a claim back to the validity & origins of appointments made thru prophets sharing the will coming from the creator.

These claims are shaky at best, and again invalidate themselves by not having thus established divine law in their own lands...

Who is the king?

So, who is the king? In recent centuries, many states have abolished the monarchy and become republics (however see, e.g., United Arab Emirates). Advocacy of government by a republic is called republicanism, while advocacy of monarchy is called monarchism. A principal advantage of hereditary monarchy is the immediate continuity of national leadership, with a usually short interregnum (as illustrated in the classic phrase "The [old] King is dead. Long live the [new] King!"). In cases where the monarch serves mostly as a ceremonial figure (e.g. most modern constitutional monarchies) real leadership does not depend on the monarch. There is further attached a host of difference between the king and a president or prime-minister, the king and the Emperor and so on...When I think of a king the term best suited in my opinion is "sovereign". Sovereign, because of the independence of subjugation to mans' law since they would be considered above it; and because of their viewed authority of divine right to rule, those who truly have ruled according to divine law have been truly slaves to serving the creator in following his will...thus I see this condition as most suitable. However; I also see this term "sovereign" and slave to the creator not only as suitable for the king, but for every man, woman and child on the earth...the king or leader is only needed for order and maintaining justice of enforcing divine law. This brings me to the point behind the mention of this chapter...

Well then why aren't each of use classified in the same suitable terms with the manifestation of tangible sovereignty in our own lives? My opinion in one word is "**LAND**". All of the wealth Kings' have comes from land ownership...from the land all things come and he/she who has land is able to truly free themselves from the shackles of modernity and the corrupt basis of the illusions of democracy which I have already shared with you. One of the arguments made by a founding participate of the Constitution was that property and ownership aren't likely in a democracy; thus the socio-economical principals it requires won't be truly representative to the masses and thus need constant reform in order to keep in moving forward until it finally implodes. Classical liberals argue that ownership and control over the means of production belongs to private firms and can only be sustained by means of consumer choice, exercised daily in the marketplace. "The capitalistic social order", they claim, therefore, "is an economic democracy in the strictest sense of the word" Critics of this claim point out that consumers only vote on the value of the *product* when they make a purchase; they are not participating in the management of firms, or voting on how the profits are to be used. Proponents of economic democracy generally argue that modern capitalism periodically results in economic crises characterized by deficiency of effective demand (which leads to surplus) and the creation of credit for manufactures to recoup some of their loses without going out of business. But still the credit may allow some purchase in advance for their surplus, but the interest based loans exceed true money circulation and thus still another dilemma lies ahead for both the creditor and debtor from receiving payment and having enough disposable income to make payments respectively; as society is unable to earn enough income to purchase its output production. Corporate monopoly of common resources typically creates artificial scarcity; in other words the rich stop spending effectively decreasing the money supply, resulting in socio-economic imbalances that restrict workers from access to economic opportunity and diminish consumer purchasing power. Economic democracy has been proposed as a component of larger socioeconomic ideologies, as a stand-alone theory, and as a variety of reform agendas.

As the world has seen its fair share of political monarchies, post legitimately appointed ones; most have sub-sided and collapsed into republic forms of government, although their practise are more of a democratic model in disguise of the ignorance people have between the republican and democratic model in rights. Most people only see it as two opposing political parties within America and understand nothing more than that…But why is it that America and her allies are always promoting this form of government ((democracy) while they themselves never intended for themselves) throughout the world, and now in defense of fascist type motives pushing NATO eastward? These two *forms* of government: Democracy and Republic, are not only dissimilar but antitheatrical, reflecting the sharp contrast between (a) The Majority Unlimited rule, in a Democracy, lacking any legal safeguard of the rights of The Individual and The Minority, and (b) The Majority Limited rule, in a Republic under a written Constitution safeguarding the rights of The Individual and The Minority. The internal tyranny of legislatures is the most formidable dread of corruption completely taken over by lobbyist groups; and repeated violations on the people have been parchment barriers committed by overbearing majorities in every state. It's beyond resolve when things have gotten so out of hand. The Republic has been stolen from the people and has now for a long time operated as a democratic model, so therefore in essence the Constitution no longer applies to the citizens. It is correct to say that in any Democracy--either a Direct or a Representative type--as a *form* of government, there can be no legal system which protects The Individual or The Minority (any or all minorities) against unlimited tyranny by The Majority. Under this *form* of government, neither the courts nor any other part of the government can effectively challenge, much less block, any action by The Majority in the legislative body, no matter how arbitrary, tyrannous, or totalitarian they might become in practice...strong indications of that are all of the ignored factions of the constitution in convictions of guilt without evidence, executive orders of assassination of citizens foreign or domestic, no longer applied habeas corpus, and patriot act, NSA / FBI policing its own citizens and the list goes on and on...Madison's observations in *The Federalist* number are noteworthy at this point because they highlight a grave error made through the centuries regarding Democracy as a *form* of government. He commented as follows:

- "Theoretic politicians, who have patronized this species of government, have erroneously supposed that by reducing mankind to a perfect equality in their political rights, they would, at the same time, be perfectly equalized and assimilated in their possessions, their opinions, and their passions."

A Republic, on the other hand, has a very different purpose and an entirely different *form*, or system, of government. Its purpose is to control The Majority strictly, as well as all others among the people, primarily to protect

The Individual's God-given, unalienable rights and therefore for the protection of the rights of The Minority, of all minorities, and the liberties of people in general. The definition of a Republic is: a constitutionally limited government of the representative type, created by a written Constitution--adopted by the people and changeable (from its original meaning) by them only by its amendment--with its powers divided between three separate Branches: Executive, Legislative and Judicial. The republic's strict adherence to the constitution that has been written in any land among its citizens that protect the rights of EVERY individual no matter what, and thus implies his or her sovereign rights to be free...One of the earliest, if not the first, specific discussions of this new American development (a Constitutional Convention) in the historical records is an entry in June 1775 in John Adams' "Autobiography" commenting on the framing by a convention and ratification by the people as follows:

- "By conventions of representatives, freely, fairly, and proportionately chosen . . . the convention may send out their project of a constitution, to the people in their several towns, counties, or districts, and the people may make the acceptance of it their own act."

Divine law frees humanity from slavery and protects their God given rights to sovereignty as each of us are inheritors of the earth in which we are born. In addition the entire creation is protected by legislation of the Creator and therefore balance is met and maintained in harmony. The Land, water, and mineral wealth are co-habittatively owned by each of us, therefore they are not commodities to be sold. None of us have created the land, water, or mineral resources; thus none of us collectively or individually have the right to sell them. Certain types of mineral deposits would be subject to taxation from fair usage if found on ones land for the larger benefit of all such as ores that could be refined into pure metals, gold, silver, lead and the like would be taxable...other deposits coal, water and the like would not. We are on the other hand are able to sell what we produce from the land excluding mineral wealth (although individual usage is allowed). These basic concepts of individual rights within divine law are closely resembled in the constitutions of Republics, which only lack the figure head that would be otherwise appointed in maintaining the justice of enforcement.

When was the republic high-jacked

It's very interesting connecting the dots, in a sort of investigative report that surely unfolds when one follows the historical link of events and the documentation that follows. In brief, I will try to enlighten everyone on the topic...

Republicanism is the guiding political philosophy of the **United States**. It has been a major part of American civic thought since its founding. It stresses *liberty* and *"unalienable" rights* as central values, makes the people as a whole sovereign, rejects aristocracy and inherited political power, expects citizens to be independent in their performance of civic duties, and vilifies corruption. Founded and put into practise in the 18 century it was intended to be the defining governance of the USA in its conception of becoming a country. An ideology to resist aristocracy (rule by the elite class), and formed on the basis of the declaration of Independence (1776), Constitution (1787) and Gettysburg address (1863). Historian Thomas Kidd (2010) had this to say:

- He argues that during the Revolution Christians linked their religion to republicanism. He states, "With the onset of the revolutionary crisis, a major conceptual shift convinced Americans across the theological spectrum that God was raising up America for some special purpose." Kidd further argues that " new blend of Christian and republican ideology led religious traditionalists to embrace wholesale the concept of republican virtue." As virtuous republicans, citizens had a growing moral obligation to eradicate the corruption they saw in the monarchy.

Historian Gordon Wood has tied the founding ideas to American Excceptionalism.

- "Our beliefs in liberty, equality, constitutionalism, and the well-being of ordinary people came out of the Revolutionary era. So too did our idea that we Americans are a special people with a special destiny to lead the world toward liberty and democracy." Americans were the protectors of liberty; they had a greater obligation and destiny to assert republican virtue.

John Adams insisted, "<u>There must be a positive Passion for the public good, the public Interest, Honor, Power, and Glory, established in the Minds of the People, or there can be no Republican Government, nor any real Liberty</u>. And this public Passion must be Superior to all private Passions. Men must be ready, they must pride themselves, and be happy to sacrifice their private Pleasures, Passions, and Interests, nay their private Friendships and dearest connections, when they stand in Competition with the Rights of society." I find it remarkably ironic the foresight that took place in the conception and choices made to eradicate the leadership of Kings' and bringing the sovereignty back to the people. Islamic law is also another system (divine law) that puts sovereignty with the people and relinquishes the tyranny of corruption. The Republican form of government was the intended goal, but understanding the comments made by John Adams, the particular proposal also had principals to follow; otherwise it would implode onto itself in hypocritical accusations of unfairness among the people, many who may have been ignorantly blind to understanding completely the comprehensiveness of its totality. John Locke has been quoted with saying, "Americans are fundamentally individualistic and not devoted to civic virtue". I think that particular quote is the culmination of attitudes or heightened exploitation of that characteristic we see widespread today.

So, when did the high-jacking occur? Well, my opinion brings me to two notions understood in the principals between the two models...

1. The Founding Fathers wanted republicanism because its principles guaranteed liberty, with opposing, limited powers offsetting one another. They thought change should occur slowly, as many were afraid that a "democracy"- by which they meant a direct democracy, would allow a majority of voters at any time to trample rights and liberties. They believed the most formidable of these potential majorities was that of the poor against the rich.

2. public Interest, Honor, Power, and Glory, established in the Minds of the People, or there can be no Republican Government, nor any real Liberty

*Keep these two statements of my opinion in mind as you read on further...

Thomas Jefferson and Albert Gallatin focused on the danger that the public debt, unless it was paid off, would be a threat to republican values. The earliest account to mention would be that of the Presidency of Alexander Hamilton who was a Federalist, not a Republican. He began to increase the national debt, which in turn directly began to threaten the republican ideals of normalcy to be maintained. Albert Gallatin who served under Both Jefferson and Madison as Secretary of Treasury, and he was now also working to lower taxes and the debt to preserve republican freedoms/ideals. Andrew Jackson was quoted as saying, "the national debt is a national curse", and he was credited with paying the entire national debt in full in 1835. Ever since this time politicians have used the national debt as a spring board to encourage stresses against the republican ideal & existence.

The Civil War of America was largely fought over economic reasons. For the South they were fight to maintain the cheap labor of slavery and the large plantations that were creating America's new wealth; For the North they were fighting for the unification of the nation...the eradication of slavery was never the priority, as the legacy of Lincoln is still told today. The emancipation proclamation was document therefore primarily to unify the country and give the slaves a reason for revolt, internal fragmentation against the south to help in their defeat. The Cotton plantations where raking in huge profits, of which the New Orleans port became a critical strategic port. Cotton was shipped via New Orleans to Europe for the production of clothing and this one product was by fair funding the south in keeping up their resistance against the North. But, after New Orleans was captured April 29, 1862 the Union through a naval action by Union forces seeking to capture the city during the American Civil War. A Union naval squadron of 43 ships under Admiral David G. Farragut entered the lower Mississippi near New Orleans and soon breached the heavy

chain cables that were stretched across the river as a prime defense.
https://en.wikipedia.org/wiki/Republicanism_in_the_United_States

For the first time in America's history citizens were required to pay federal income tax to fund the war. Salmon P. Chase, Lincoln's Treasury Secretary oversaw the first federal currency and national banking system in 1863. The standardized currency allowed the United States to issue $500 million in war bonds, with the banks providing a market for them. The bonds were primary created to give value to the newly created federal notes giving them financial backing. After the war was over the government insisted on paying back the war debt and thus called in all then labeled "greenback"; this resulted in the longest deflationary period in American history. After labor revolts, and other economically related stresses, to prevent such a thing from happening in the future the country adopted the gold standard in 1900...Three types:

1. Gold specie standard, associated with the value of circulating gold coins
2. Gold Bullion standard, sold bullion on demand at fixed prices in exchanges for circulating currency.
3. Gold exchange, government guarantees a fixed exchange rate to the currency of another country that also uses a gold standard regardless of the notes used in exchange representing the gold.

The economic warfare prior to WWI began to cause countries to abandon or suspend their gold standards...basically a manipulation of finance to determine the enduring opponents of the war, since World Wars also cause shifts of power & influence. The ruling state at the time was held by Britain...According to Lawrence Officer the main cause of the gold standard's failure to resume its previous position after World War 1 was "the Bank of England's precarious liquidity position of the gold-exchange standard." A run on sterling caused Britain to impose exchange controls that fatally weakened the standard, although convertibility wasn't legally suspended. But, Gold prices were no longer the same in playing the roles they had prior. Manipulation of the market was the games played on the commodity...Gold is a commodity that for 1000yrs has virtually kept a stable value unchanged unless direct manipulation through politics is applied. By 1914 and 1915 the trade surplus in America exceeded $1 billion dollars for the first time. Not able to recover quickly enough, the country soon fell in the "Great Depression", which killed the gold standard completely. Gold specie (circulated gold) was then replaced with Gold bullion, which the British Empire & bank of England are accredited. But, get this they would return back to the gold standard in 1925 in conjunction with Australia and South Africa in repealing the gold species and introducing the bullion standard with the British Gold Standard Act of 1925. But again, the Great Depression killed the Standard altogether (1929-1933). In these vulnerable years there were numerous runs on currencies that threatened their futures.

The advent of the Federal Reserve Bank came about but, it was prevented initially from expanding the money supply from the adherence to the gold standard; but once the gold standard was killed it became free in money creation.

- The **Federal Reserve Act** (Ch. 6, 38 Stat. 251, enacted December 23, 1913, 12 U.S.C. Ch. 3) is an Act of Congress that created and established the Federal Reserve System, the central banking system of the United States, and granted it the legal authority to issue Federal Reserve Notes (now commonly known as the U.S. Dollar) and Federal Reserve Bank Notes as legal tender. The Act was signed into law by President Woodrow Wilson. http://www.thefiscaltimes.com/Articles/2011/04/12/Civil-War-at-150-Debt-Lessons-from-Lincoln

Created well in advance it seems that this premeditated conspiracy would be purposely implemented after forth coming events that would allow it to be enacted. The pieces of the puzzle are many, and the positions of presidents, cabinet members, congress, and other well placed people within key roles would systematically sabotage the Republic. Fast forward a century and a half to see how the country took a somewhat different approach to its finances during the Iraq and Afghanistan Wars. In 2003, just two months after the U.S. invaded Iraq, Congress passed the second round of what has become known as the Bush tax cuts, which lowered income tax rates, as well as levies on investment income (the first was passed in 2001, before 9/11). The unfolding wars were then funded predominantly by assuming higher levels of federal debt, leaving the U.S. today $14.3 trillion in the hole as of 2011. Therefore, in conclusion the monetary sabotage of America has been the main catalyst in comprising the sovereignty of the Republic and its citizens. However, this conspiracy by far out-stretches just the American community but has become an international policy of mainly the western philosophy to entrap humanity into subdued oppression. The blood sucking like craving needed to feed its survival is the validity it carries to subjugate the world...and if anyone was to research further into the depths of Free-masonry you would surely uncover even deeper conspiracies scripted prior that explain further the events that have occurred with the consequences we have witnessed to date. Frighteningly accurate, it smashes the conspiracy portion of the claim to most, giving it a definitive affirmation of a political agenda being carried out to the letter...

Philosophical / political majority vs minority

Unfortunately, the world is collapsing into this dynamic of a new human psyche...associations not based on true bonds or friendships, but rather on associative positions & groupings. These are the defining points of human interaction today...

Now, along with these associations & groupings comes a philosophy that it carries...a life or mission statement of a large company at directing its participants towards the foreseen goal. Within that lies a culture to be adhered to, and acts as a sort of recognition of one member to the next, like a uniform if you will. This is very important as each member, in part of our human nature, is vulnerable to the need of being liked or fitting in. Therefore the ground is set for the rhetoric that is to be sold in maintaining the captive minds to a philosophy that perpetuates the mission statement into the future towards it goals. Rhetoric, largely biased philosophy with a political twist is the jargon that it is used or heard over and over. Now, this is solely my opinion when I pondered over the elite and the corporate media of America...It's so redundantly absurd, and full of holes, without intentionally insulting anyone, you really have to be quite behind the curve to fall for most of what is said. Education hasn't changed much in its curriculum in nearly 50yrs, with all the other distractions set in place to further people from the truth, the TV has become a hypnotic device with redundant chatter given around the clock. Radio is another big one...hour on the hour, the selection of what is played takes over the minds of our young people as they become more distant & careless. These political groupings lie at the very heart of this battle between the hearts and minds of the people today.

Of course, this particular ideology has very far reaching effects, as we see the culture and influence of America beamed around the world. This exporting factors of music, athletics, actor/actresses, brands, and celebrity promote the influence of America onto the rest of the world thousands of miles away.

Nationalism, racism, gender, class, education, culture/religion even sexual orientations are all topics of bias that are fragmenting society. Although I enjoy at times good philosophical discussions, I make it a habit to knot involve philosophy into critical issues. Defined as a rational investigation of the truths & principals of being, knowledge, or conduct...it often lacks sound conclusion and almost always robustness to overlooked variables. In my opinion it's also full of doubt as every point is subject to ifs of but's... within its own definition lies the investigation of knowledge, which raises the red flag or barrier of its application. Philosophy is the politics of people or groups, who are aligned along the same principals and conduct thus it is highly subject to prejudice from person to person, group to group. It is a killer of faith altogether, as it often questions things above human comprehension, and it's usually the ingredient of interpretation which, has deviated many people in adapting alternate versions of pure doctrine. Human desires to change things to benefit their particular taste or enhancement is something of a disease in seeing the wrong behind such actions, but philosophy has a way of causing people to believe things given somewhat a logical interpretation or explanation especially when knowledge is lacked overall.

Ignorance is the driving force behind much of today's politics...foreign policy, false-flag operations, media propaganda and television coverage all play into the tricks of confusion and manipulation of what people think. Public opinion is thus controlled by professional rhetoric as much of what is true is buried in deceit. This classification has created many groups, but the two main groups of the majority vs minority have most control over the influence of conditions. The gap of wealth in America created long ago, has threatened the freedom of those who still struggle for the American nightmare as I call it since the struggle is never pleasant. Wealth & illegal business control America and control the daily lives of the people. Nothing is shielded from the temptations of money from the presidential elections to the average person's loyalty to means of immorality due to hardships incurred otherwise. In fact, just about everyone would justify some immoral sustenance in means of feeding their families in America rather than by trying to eradicate the corruption altogether by one sound voice. Can't beat'em..join'em ... I know things have gotten worse and the economic struggles that we face, but we really have to ask ourselves how have these things gotten so bad? Government isn't apart from us; instead it's an extension of ourselves. As much as I hate to say it, Government is a reflection of the people and its character period... Overly opinionated & uneducated on critic issues; and too much useful energy applied to mundane affairs...Second hand knowledge of only what is broadcasted or interpreted for you, so very easily misled and misguided from minor to life changing events. Without delving into the subject to far; one recent example would be 911...Now, as tragic as things were on that dreadful day; there has come after it so much evidence debunking the lies told by then President Bush, media, and the congressional investigation as well as I witnesses from the NYP, NYFD, survivors, engineers, security guards that worked in the Trade center and the list goes on (https://www.youtube.com/watch?v=kuRTXRBB5Vo) ...that have all concurred to the implosion of demolitions etc. Militarily investigations have slowly been breaking wind to disclose the pre-speech of such an event occurring by the likes of Secretary of State Codelessa Rice, and others in addition to soldiers station at NORAD (North America Aerospace Defense Command) http://www.vanityfair.com/news/2006/08/norad200608 being told to stand down. The planes that flew into the twin towers had flight paths of over an hour and were witnessed by NORAD who dispatched fighter jets who could have engaged but instead were told otherwise. Lastly, the supposed hijackers passports were found among all the burning debris etc. but they themselves had surfaced in their own countries, one gave a press conference in Morocco on the BBC, but the American press especially ignored it as to keep the path with the implanted lie they were propagating. Now, as a result to all this American politics, its economy, military spending, and still proceeding imperialism has ensued in the middle-east and now Eastern Europe. Unable to believe that a government is able to carry out such a thing on its own people is beyond most and those who have bought into this monstrous lies are those who have also pledged their loyalties to the ongoing hegemony of America by any means necessary. This small group of people are able to buy a larger group from the minority in order to make themselves the majority while creating a defense minority subject to their "mob rule", but who stand to not buy into their lies. The philosophy of America's greatness, god bless her and no one else etc. is a dead speech revived with newly invented words of terror, justification of democracy etc. in wake or testimony of foreigners who have also been flipped to the same, inclining more thoughts of people into believing what is seriously not true. "Your either with us or against us", as Bush Jr. would say...this is literally the line drawn in the dirt and people have been taking sides all around the world.

Hypocrisy as become very common place with spies and watchful eyes implanted everywhere to gather information as well as infiltrate in order to further steer their agenda to its intended goal. This has taken its effect on the relationships between people & driven the wedge of fragmentation even further. Whatever bears material gain, or the truth lies with the number of people gathered on a common agreeance, and or the ability to change things with modernity that have been throughout history seen as evil or abominations...these are the sickness of modernity and the "Obey your Thirst" nation of followers of philosophical excuses that are very shallow in legitimising the actions of some people.

Battle between the sexes

Widely unexplainable in definitive terms to dynamic characteristics of human-beings conditioned and sensitized by their respective environments & other societal influences...but one thing is for certain the relationship between the sexes has definitely changed. For the better or the good, you ask? Well, my opinion would be for the worst, although that condition of "worse" varies depending on where you are in the world. But, let's say for terms of clarity...let's base the premise from an American standard since they are the leading nation in the world. So, unless otherwise mentioned the premise will be assumed on the American model. In addition, this isn't an attempt to nor do I see it as an opportunity to attack America. I on the contrary don't see collectively in all things but rather individually as it applies to the collective. Therefore, each individual has a responsibility to the collective, and it's only when those singularly responsibilities are neglected does the collective suffer.

This first thing that comes to mind when I consider the topic is marriage, and how many of the marriages are successful. Healthy marriages are usually a good catalyst to understanding the overall picture between men & woman...in addition to what our eyes show & tell us while were out and about.

Worldwide Divorce Rates ""Top 20 Countries with Highest Divorce Rates/ Capita

1. Belarus 68%
2. Russian Federation 65%
3. Sweden 64%
4. Latvia 63%
5. Ukraine 63%
6. Czech Republic 61%
7. Belgium 56%
8. Finland 56%
9. Lithuania 55%
10. United Kingdom 53%
11. Moldova 52%

12. United States 49%
13. Hungary 46%
14. Canada 45%
15. Norway 43%
16. France 43%
17. Germany 41%
18. Netherlands 41%
19. Switzerland 40%
20. Iceland 39%
21. Kazakhstan 39%

Many current divorce statistics studies estimate that the divorce rate in the United States is hovering right around 50%, with nearly half of all marriages ending in divorce. In an international study of countries with the highest divorce rates, the U.S. takes its spot at Number 12 with a 49% divorce rate, and just about as close to 50% as you can get (*Huffington Post, 2014*). The Huffington post suggests that the divorce rate isn't really at 50 percent -- and it isn't really rising either; In fact, a new piece in the New York Times' data blog Upshot suggests that the divorce rate has actually been *dropping* for some time now. Looking at the numbers, the Times suggest the high divorce rate of the late 1970s and early 1980s may have just been a "historical anomaly," rather than a trend (http://www.huffingtonpost.com/2014/12/02/divorce-rate). Be that as it may in contradiction to opposing polls; another fact is that should be consider in the reduction of divorce is the sheer lack of marriage...I know that this is case especially among black woman in America, who I have often heard quoted in saying," there aren't enough good black-men around to choose from". In addition to the availability remains the question of standards being sought by these women who are for the most part more educated than their black-men counterparts. Of-course the branches sprout out in all directions bearing even more fruitful reasons in predictions on each newly exposed condition. Education is probably one of the most widely used "contemporary" reasons they would call it...as to say that the science between man/woman has evolved to a higher more sophisticated state...but keep that on the mind while we finish the first point on education.

Sure, when you refer back to the top 20 countries with the highest divorce rate you see mainly developed, western countries...these countries in the modernity and contemporary status place such high emphasis on education because of the need to compete in the job market to keep up with the ever advancing cost of living. This goes beyond opinion and falls on the basis of fact; in fact this particular concept of maintaining this system of progression is locked in perpetual incline for the very nature of this system follows a very strict principal and thus; in order for a democracy To maintain their power, these candidates must adopt an ever-increasing tax and spend policy to satisfy the ever-increasing desires of the majority. As taxes increase, incentive to produce decreases, causing many of the once productive to drop out and join the non-productive; When there are no longer enough producers to fund the legitimate functions of government and the socialist programs, the democracy will collapse, always to be followed by a Dictatorship. This is the cusp the America finds herself today...what else explains the heightened police state of America, and all of their outrageous actions resulting in so many deaths of black citizens? Not to mention the implementation of Jad helm 15 and other pre-martial law practices taking place around the country reading those to impose it. *(http://sayyarismail.weebly.com/blog-country-or-corporation), 2015.* So, with this "contemporary" type sophistication comes governing principals that must be maintain to feed this perpetuated cycle of want by successive generations in transfer of previous generations in the job market handover. This political case in point directly affects one of the most widely used factors in divorce and or in considering qualified candidates, because the burden of sustenance is placed so high. Spinning off of that particular principal further it becomes easy to see how that one underlying principal to maintain that sort of society affects & degrades the family unit, introduces the need for two-parent income house-holds, under attended to children exposing them to the dangers of trouble earlier, depopulation of particular ethnic groups who make up the majority in those countries, and the lack of quality time spent between individuals in sustaining longevity in relationships. The implications are very; very heavy as to the domino affect it has throughout the overall infrastructure and well-being of a family, community, city, state, and or nation...

One well known human trait is we all are more comfortable with those we can identify with...difference aren't so much the compulsion to know one another initially anymore, but rather are more of a repellant. The societal pressures of affiliation and status often weigh so heavily on ones choices that it is disregarded clearly, and conquered by the opinions of maintaining those social groups. Now, of course I'm not categorizing the entire human populace or the subjects of these stats in America; but it definitely has enough merit to mention here as a mechanism of hindrance. Fraternities and high society type pledges usually seek out one another in trying to maintain that status post-college and into early adult-hood. So, it's clearly that college educated peoples usually initially look to fulfill that desire 1st.

In contrast to education are those who never go onto higher learning...The un-educated group (which I tend to believe the entitlement of "un-educated" never applies to anyone who is applying themselves in some regard) tend to marry sooner in life. The high-school sweetheart cases etc... Of which, many or even most, I would be opinionated to say, have very successful and delightful tales of their struggles, which has caused them to bond like only they can. I would further say that this particular group makes up the majority of the people in the world. Happy with what they have for the most part, although better means may be something sought; they don't have any regard to such restriction in having children, and see divorce as something that is more so life threatening as a plays a toll on the ability to exist. Fundamentally built on the basis of community and existence of the unit; it's a replica of our early existence with tribal implication. Today, due to economic depression and scarcity of jobs, many college graduates are beginning to see the humble nature of tradesmen's and such are able to go out an hustle up a livelihood on skills that may have been passed down from fathers, uncles, etc. previously without the high-interest based loans needed to attend college. Women, who previously overlooked these men, are too again beginning to re-recognize the less-stressful and ease of these men to earn a modest living. While others who see the world only through means of material gain and status are forced into interracial marriages as the alternate option. I myself, don't stand opposed to interracial anything, however in America with all of its tense, racial relations from day one I don't see how any interracial marriage can truly be happy with so much persisted bigotry nation-wide. Sure, there will be exceptions but the majority will ultimately fall victim to aggression and other stresses that are sure to strain the strongest marriages...

That being said so far, in brief exploring only that of education mainly, the complex combinations for successful relationships that flourish instead of withering away are complex indeed. But the model that the world is based on mostly is the uneducated model that they tend to marry sooner etc. and it's this model that makes up the majority of the world. Deriving from the aspect of a necessity for continuation to life rather than just reproduction; we see that the countries for majority people of color to reside don't show up among the top 20 countries of the developed western countries. That speaks volumes, and should be a standard on which humanity plots a trend back towards. But, as the capitalistic, democratic model is to be maintained with a forever trending populace in increased spending (as man is never satisfied in his desires) the appetite of later generations has continued on an unchecked balance-sheet for decades now...Agreeable with only the enjoyable emotions of Joy, mirth, vanity, incentives towards personal desires, music, dancing, wine, and good cheer...he's has become abhorrent towards the opposites... life is surely to bring i.e. sorrow, melancholy, poverty, and humility. Therefore, he has become drunk on seeking to maintain certain aspects of life that are impossible and not meant in this life, although that notion plays into deeper moral beliefs. "You only have one life to live", and "obey your thirst"; are in fact slogans that encourage and try to bring legitimacy to seeking & sustaining the former emotions by all efforts rather than teaching people to strike a happy medium. The cylindrical cycle of life and experience is mathematically not possible in sustaining constant felicity in this world...That is not so hard to understand really by just applying the most basic of common sense.

A good Segway into the love and hate mixture of human affections all conditioned by pop-culture. For a few decades now, the culture of America has been trying to condition its own citizen's black, white, and other as to what the typical relationship and or house-hold should be. From the 1970's family shows of the Walton's, Little House on the Prairie, Brady Bunch, Happy Days for white-folks but also meant for other racial ethnic groups in selling the imagery of white-folks to others in adaptation and superiority...to Shows like What's happening, Good Times, Sanford & Son, The Jefferson, Different Strokes, and even Fat Albert for black folks...all of these shows depicted a range of emotions on the spectrum and taught an element of humility as the basic underlying themes. But, as time progressed, the subtle temperature increase of the boiling water went un-noticed & barely felt. As the wealth of white-folks rose so did the haughtiness of their respective shows; while blacks shows now depicted professional families no longer struggling such as "the Huxtables" with Bill Cosby. These influences have been very successful in conditioning the minds and the realities of so many Americans to date. Although nearly 60 percent of the U.S. population was labeled middle class by the mid-1950s, 25 percent of all families and more than 50 percent of two-parent Black families were poor... So, as the affluence of ethnic groups has increased, so has the status in how each has been depicted in the media. These same conditions have become the forever adjusting upward trend that we see affecting society as a whole. The upward movement isn't an indication of becoming better; rather it is the opposite indication of society worsening. Studiously avoiding prevalent social issues such as racial discrimination and civil rights, the shows focused on mostly White middle-class families with traditional nuclear roles (mother in the home, father in the office) and implied that most complicated domestic problems could be solved within a 30-minute time slot, always ending with a strong moral lesson. From the humility of the earlier shows broadcasters' have demonstrated their power to influence viewers, either consciously through slanted political commentary, or subtly, by portraying controversial relationships (such as single parenthood, same-sex marriages, or interracial couplings) as socially acceptable. The symbiotic nature of television and culture is exemplified in every broadcast, from family sitcoms to serious news reports. These influences in turn further curb the decision processes of young-adults in the marriage preferences.

But, how as this affected younger generations? Ah, the meat & potatoes of the topic I like to refer to it...as the yard stick is pulled out to measure just how humanity has drifted in this infinite relationship man has with his companion. Now, more or less a hybrid between music, film and sports there's virtually nothing in the broadcast rotation not designed to market and sell this new American-idol type existence that is seemingly duplicated in every culture around the world. (http://2012books.lardbucket.org/books/culture-and-media/s12-02-the-relationship-between-telev.html).

Services such as Cable News Network (CNN), Entertainment and Sports Programming Network (ESPN), and Music Television (MTV) profoundly altered the television landscape in the world of news, sports, and music. New markets opened up for these innovative program types, as well as for older genres such as the sitcom. Shows such as these began to tap into the emotions of viewers, and for our younger viewers emotions are heavily influential upon person development. Creatures' of habit, and duplication it has effectively cloned younger persons in adapting TV personalities into their own identities. Each seeking his or her acceptance into society, duplication of personalities popularized by TV popularity easily become the bench mark standard many youth began to take on. Soon, these attitudes and personas were visible in the schools, in the mall, and gathering spots...Culture was now experiencing a huge swing of the pendulum towards a youth based, new generation movement that wouldn't only effect television, but go onto change everything from music, English-language, fashion, and food. By the late 70's even black families (especially in the industrialized north) began to cross-over into the middle-class income bracket. Speaking from my own experiences mainly, and from what I myself witnessed...I call it the last era of the black family unit. The 1970's were the last 10 years that most black families in my region of the north-east remained a two-parent unit. In my case, up until the Michael Jackson "Off the Wall Album" was released, 1972 with 5 pending years of parental adjudication before the final decision would be made. By the time the decision was made...another cultural change was slowly pushing itself into play.

The hip/hop culture

It would seem also that by the 1970's the black-man in America had reached is economical heights and was now again threatening the seat of superiority by his white captures now well prompted up from slave labor, and the then new industrialized push of demand for machinery in supplying WW1 efforts of the British. Long seeking to have what the white-man had the black-man post slavery had been duped out of the land grants awarded after slavery. The 13, 14, 15 amendments to the constitution, which many question there ratification...have done very little at protecting the rights of black folks. In addition, to that not seeing the finely honed in skilled trades many had carried over from slavery they mostly sought to give them up for secularized education, which many had benefited from in the "great migration" to the north to work in the factories...the slavery of servitude in the South with now pay, and worse than animal like conditions in regard...to a slavery of dependency in the North by employment. The inheritance of the slave in the land he was given was the freedom that should have been maintained, for by it surely would freedom be sustained.

But, the 70's would bring about America's defeat in the Viet Nam War, and a returning of G.I's, many whom were black, along with it a paralleled national epidemic of Heroine to go with it...1865 to 1965 with a few more years to boast still with racial hardships; the black-man would now be plotted against in another conspiracy to take him backwards in which, he would never regain the fullness of consciousness.

It's like a jungle sometimes it makes me wonder
How I keep from going under
It's like a jungle sometimes it makes me wonder
How I keep from going under

Broken glass everywhere
People pissing on the stairs, you know they just don't care
I can't take the smell, I can't take the noise no more
Got no money to move out, I guess I got no choice
Rats in the front room, cockroaches in the back
Junkie's in the alley with a baseball bat
I tried to get away, but I couldn't get far
'Cause a man with a tow-truck repossessed my car

Chorus:
Don't push me cause I'm close to the edge
I'm trying not to lose my head, ah huh-huh-huh
[2nd and 5th: ah huh-huh-huh]

(LYRICS FROM Mellie Mel, Grand Master Flash & and the Furious Five)

 The lyrics paint the back-drop of the new social plummet of black-people post 1960's civil-rights movements and Vietnam. From a seemingly fair means of sustenance achieved by a few in reaching the middle class in the northern factories & businesses; This societal level within the African American community that primarily began to develop in the early 1960s, when the ongoing African-American Civil Rights Movement led to the outlawing of _de jure_ racial segregation. The gains accrued by the Civil Rights Era were strongly correlated with the emergence of a new black middle class. Specifically defined with-in the lower-

middle class or working class; In terms of income $3,100 to $62,000 while yet another view projects $20,000 to $100,000, but these figures are more aligned to more recent years in projections. In the 1960's only 43% of whites completed high school where in contrast the black population 20% with only 3% finishing college. Now, a sharp left turn into the decadence of multiple national recessions that occurred in the 1970's and 80's directly impacted the Black community. These recessive years also targeted the many social aiding programs that were gained during civil rights in order to equalize the playing field for Blacks…now were seen as burdensome and therefore their legitimacy was attacked. These institutions fell under scrutiny well into the housing bubble years of 2006 which, further depleted minority wealth…Poverty among the

black community was from  31.3% in 1976 to 27.2% in 2014, according to census data. By comparison, the overall U.S. poverty rate has increased from 12.3% in 1976 to 14.9% in 2014. So, if these numbers are true without getting to analytical about stats…over 38 yrs. and increase in the poverty percentage of only 4.1% tells me that the majority of black folks have been basically held very tightly grouped within the same framework. It doesn't seem like much when looked at by itself; but when it's compared In contrast with a 3% overall national rate for all other racial groups for the same period of time it speaks volumes…This dependency on the economy without any independence as a community to self-produce and self-sustain, the black community recessed into perpetual regression with the increased number of lost jobs. The automation process of many industrial type jobs was another big hit, with the overall lack of disposable income from other Americans', which many of these production lines relied on demographically.

But the real killer to the community was something much more sinister…For a long time; many people have believed that African-Americans were targeted by the Central Intelligence Agency to receive the cocaine which decimated black communities in the 1980s. In 1979 Congress held rushed hearings into the perils of cocaine and was told, time and again by expert after expert that cocaine was not a problem because it was not seriously addictive, too expensive and not easy to find. The hearings, chaired by Republican Congressman Tennyson Guyer in the House Select Committee on Narcotics Abuse and Control did not live up to Guyer's hopes of finding a devil in the drug cocaine. Only one man, Dr. Robert Byck of Yale University was insistent that trouble was coming and it was BIG trouble. Byck was a professor of psychiatry and pharmacology at Yale Medical School. He began his testimony by stating, "What I would like to talk to you about for the most part is the importance of telling the truth... We have given a great deal of cocaine to many individuals and find it to be a most unremarkable drug." "For about a year, a Peruvian police psychiatrist named Dr. Raul Jeri had been insisting that wealthy drug users in Lima were being driven insane by cocaine. A psychiatrist in Bolivia, Dr. Nils Noya, began making similar claims shortly thereafter." What had been discovered was an addiction so overwhelming that middle and upper class students and middle class wage earners in Peru and Bolivia had abandoned every aspect of a normal human life, including eating, drinking, personal hygiene to the point of defecating in clothes that would remain unchanged for days, family and shelter in the pursuit of "basuco". Basuco is one of the first stages of the pasting cocoa leaves...and this is the reaction to the base of the drug, not yet to mention the genesis of the drug into its form of rocking it that would be sold to the black community. These pioneering doctors were ignored & encountered nothing but resistance from the government. By the time the government was compelled to acknowledge that cocaine smoking had reached the U.S., and that it was having a devastating effect, the experts, including Siegel and Byck, who were now warning of an epidemic of near biblical proportions... Furthermore, the Food and Drug Administration shut down attempts to do any serious research on addiction or treatment, refusing to approve grant requests or research proposals and withholding government permits necessary to run experiments with controlled substances.

(http://www.fromthewilderness.com/free/pandora/blacks-targeted.html).

"Just say "NO" to drugs", Reagan-omics and covert wars found funding in supplying the black community with drugs. The incredibly, successful, commercialized propaganda of the epidemic that was now plaguing the urban inner-cities of America...cleverly distinguished, it was implemented at the naiveté of the American people that their own government could & would stoop to such low tactics of selling drugs in order to fund its covert agendas. This drug network opened the first pipeline between Colombia's cocaine cartels and the black neighborhoods of Los Angeles, a city now known as the "crack" capital of the world. The cocaine that flooded in helped spark a crack explosion in urban America . . . and provided the cash and connections needed for L.A.'s gangs to buy automatic weapons. Made possible by Oscar Danilo Blandon and Norwin Meneses; two individuals with ties to the Fuerza Democratica Nicaraguense (FDN), one group comprising the Nicaraguan Contras. Blandon and Meneses reportedly sold tons of cocaine to Freeway Ricky Ross, who in turn converted it to crack and sold it in the black communities of South Central Los Angeles. Blandon and Meneses were said to have used their drug trafficking profits to help fund the Contra army's war effort. Security Council and CIA had approved the use of heroin smuggled through Kurdestan, as a means of (re)arming the Kurds to fight against Saddam Hussein in 1975.The poppies plants of Afghanistan during the C.I.A's covert, proxy war against then Soviet Union, was harvested and processed to produce some of the purest heroine to hit the streets...Successful on the cold-war front, and in the coups taking place in south America, the C.I.A. & the USA government found it beneficial in the ability to by-pass congress for covert funds...and at the same time decimate the black community. By the time anyone caught onto the operation, it had reached extremely high heights of success. An implanted a virus that our own black people would begin to spread among their own people;

Incredible, the shift of momentum that was taking place; and this shift was drastically changing the over-al landscape of the community it was also affecting the black male and female relations in the black community especially in the areas affected the most in the beginning...The attitudes of people also began to shift from the love of family to the selfishness of individuals. It was as if things happened so quickly in getting bad that no one understood what, how, or why, so they blamed each other. This wedge, already well aimed and politically in position, was beginning to be driven into the community and it's been driven deeper & deeper ever since...

In the north-east the culture rapidly taking root in representing the younger generation of off-spring from the Motown era...was by large just a happy past time & creative arts type genre of musical expression. But by the later 1970's & early 1980's a political consciousness began to creep up into the body of lyrics and continued to grow in all direction of self-articulation. The political problems of the inner-city found an outlet that in the beginning connected every inner-city housing project around the country. The music solely owned by the young black youth began to make a statement that would be along the likes of lyrics made my late, great Bob Marley. A newly created form of activism through a new form of musical expression...Extremely versatile & robust it was not only a forum of entertainment, but a source of awakening all packaged into the same 3-5mins. Music, and it's extremely effective ability to move people of all walks of life was again being used towards activism. Not yet upon the international stage, it spoke to the specific problems going on in the black neighborhoods across America largely unknown to the white population. The consciousness grew, and grew until more formal, informative groups formed like public Enemy, who took a more direct Malcolm X type of approach in speech. Heavily impacted beyond expectations, I might add, it fueled and lit a young black political movement unseen since the death of prominent leaders in the 1960's. The culture had now reached and filled a very big void that had plagued the black community for 20yrs up to that point. The red, black, and green movement of young black people wearing African necklaces, clothing, hats...even among the woman they were wearing their hair more natural or in braids. The level of the activism was constantly rising and aligning the black man in America to his ancestry in the African continent. In the 60's Malcom X after his Hajj to Mecca and African tour, he returned to America but with speeches that were calling black people to re-align with Africa. Many African leaders were willing to aide Malcolm financially in his work, and this became very, very dangerous...the movement died with the assassinations of him and Martin Luther King Jr. and would remain dead until re-awoken with this hip new movement. New blood that was pure to the commitment, younger, and angered after 20yrs of abuse since the loses of the 60's...it was again a force that needed to be dealt with and if so subdued.

Largely, modeled after the Black Panther party (*the political group formed by Huey P. Newton whereby they would police & protect the affairs of the black community instead of the outside police)*, the lyrics where as controversial as could be...but like anything black giving significance to a legitimate call or need; its momentum was curved from that of changing the government to the shady business dealing of black artist in selling their art by the mid 1990's. Thus began the subduing of the political movement, which would then turn from the consciousness of East Coast hip hop to the gangster-ism of the new L.A. based genre that was emerging. Unlike, its counter-part on the East...this movement still embodied the wrongs of police and state towards blacks, but the more subtle exploitation was that hinged on the anger element. More violent physically, with syndicate drug trade ties this new gangster image would be marketed both positively & negatively smothering the consciousness that was the formable target. Robbed of its intelligence, it was left with only the anger which was redirected from where it was needed to the community itself. Black on black crime would surge and all of a sudden appealing to another generation called "X" it become cool to kill your own kind with malicious gun-play flooding the streets of L.A.

From the west distribution channels would move eastward into virtually every inner-city urban city east to Kansas and would then later topple over into white suburbia as white-new generation X'ers would adopt the music and movement. Hip hop would never again have a mainstream political voice as most consciousness artist are not heard on the radio; instead hour after hour the most degrading, reverse propaganda is shared on the airwaves degrading the youth further into self-annihilation… This new gangster-ized movement was exactly what the racial politics needed to drive the nail into the coffin in moving this agenda forward. The adaption of the gangster to illegal drug sells etc. had found its salesman whom many used rap music as a front in claiming monies, cars, & homes without paper trails to account for anything.

The increased gang violence brought an epidemic of black killings and inspired movies like boyz N'da hood…Unfortunately the message was smothered with glamourized other aspects that were more appealing to the viewers. A sort of hypocrisy in the film itself, that was by far outweighed in sustain the negative aspect rather than the positive.

Relative to their numbers in the general population and among drug offenders, black Americans are disproportionately arrested, convicted, and incarcerated on drug charges. The drug of principal concern was crack cocaine, erroneously believed to be a drug used primarily by black Americans. The use of cocaine, primarily powder cocaine, had increased in the late 1970s and early 1980s, particularly among whites, but powder cocaine use did not provoke the "orgy of media and political attention" from 1980's smokable form of cocaine appeared. Although the use of crack was by no means limited to low-income, urban, minority neighborhoods, it was those neighborhoods which more visibly suffered from crack addiction, and the nuisance and violence that accompanied the struggle of different drug-dealing groups to establish control over its distribution in the 1980s and 1990s. Crack in black neighborhoods was a politician's key topic for a complicated and deep-rooted set of racial, class, political, social, and moral dynamics. Politicians were able to woo a white electorate anxious about its declining status through the race-coded language of "drugs" and "crime." One interesting aspect to take particular note of was cocaine in the black community allowed state officials to regain control over these communities who were to some degree working automatously.

Published in the Stanford Law and Policy Review June 19, 2009
(https://www.hrw.org/news/2009/06/19/race-drugs-and-law-enforcement-united-states)

The race to incarcerate in the Reagan and Busch years has helped to make America the world's leading country in % of incarcerated citizens...in a seemingly just and developed society. A society that is literally exported and marketed throughout the world in selling the carbon paper to becoming a carbon-copy of a very troubled and illusionary society... (http://www.truth-out.org/opinion/item/16065-ronald-reagan-made-the-war-on-drugs-a-race-to-incarcerate). This glamourized false existence of a bi-lateral depiction isn't known by the buying foreign populace made to fantasize about a life in America. Unrealistic, the dream has a night-mare component that overshadows the quality of sleep needed first to have a dream...only while fast asleep can those willing participants seek or should I say hope for the kind of dream they fantasized about since dreams aren't controlled by any of us.

We have been for told about the greatness of democratic society, its beauty in choices etc. but it's all done so on the idealism of the notions and the ignorance of those who buy into these ideals already half duped to sleep. This mob type rule where the majority control the minority; has been tainted with the element of greed disguised within the terminology of modernity, capitalistic societies bent towards consumption, and do as you please incentives towards fulfilling the bottom-less void of desires...This trap of very seasoned lowly human, carnal desire devoid of self-discipline is the call of today's global order, which those inclined aren't able to see past the forth-coming consequences of the choices made today. Thus, the majority have acquired this perception of immorality & irresponsible means to the collective and see the modern model with its perceived eases as something of evolutionary progression. This particular marketing campaign has been very effective across demographic lines unfortunately, with even groups prone to alienation or disenfranchisement buying in to the rhetoric as smaller material gains not given to them as a whole are gained by a few individuals. This in turn has been used as a larger bargaining tool for the majority of disenfranchised to second-guess the reality cloaked by sell-outs helping to turn others to the dark side of backward momentum where everything previous will be forfeited indefinitely...All the sacrifices of life & liberty lost and without any shame as men and women a nation of people have lost their identity, but more importantly, they have lost all respect national and internationally because they have relinquished or better yet sold their DIGNITY...

Black woman/black man

What's the difference between black men/women in America and or even Africa compared to the ethnicity of any other similar group severely oppressed like say, the Palestinians? In my opinion, the difference is they have not taken out of context the roles men and women play in society...from that root, sourced perception spring boards a host of other relevant things that helps struggling people stay ground even during the toughest of times. Yes, to the credit of the African-American (who should drop the American connotation & reunify his/herself with the mother Africa), no other people has systemically and successfully been stripped of identity, language, religion, origins etc. in the history of the world as they were. This very long period of subjugation still has a few centuries to endure by the Palestinians to catch up with those ignored sufferings. In no attempt to discredit in the promotion of the other...I merely voice these facts and opinions from myself. But a lot is to be learned when superimposing one onto the other. The Palestinians efforts still in their infant years of subjugation as compared to the transatlantic slave trade and massacre; but the starting points are very similar in their resistance...deeply religious both sought death over object service thru oppression; unbreakable in that spirit they died making a stand or where awarded return. Others never gave up the fight in becoming free again through longer processes of buying their freedoms through long years of service. The African people and their ability to survive such ordeals is truly a testament to their strength and therefore should be regarded today as a motivational factor. It is of course regarded by the enemy, and I believe it's the underlying reason why so many are imprisoned or otherwise murdered to keep the masses of those numbers in-able to fight for a common cause. Physically strong in stature, the problems lie within the fractured mindset of the former slave. Hatred of self which is also projected outward upon other subjects of the same ethnicity and background; this hatred underlines the cohesion of the people as a whole. Diseased, in every way made possible, and kept starved for societal gains, as well as individual appetites...this keeps black folks carelessly, wondering in wilderness, unable to identify with himself by recognition of his brother or sister who also suffers the same conditions. You would hope to see old tactics and manipulations die off, but somehow they have been perpetuated subtlety to later generations often with worse consequences. How so, one might ask? Well, my opinion is through the relationship between the black man and woman.

Unlike other racial ethnicities, black woman have been targeted and exploited tremendously by stripping them of beauty, worth, status, and pride by subjecting them to:

- the demotion of beauty in contrast to other woman
- De-moralizing her through imagery depicting her as only a sex object with degrading speech et.
- Historical records, and her past greatness otherwise overlooked and portrayed by other ethnic woman in roles; as well as for the black men played by white actors.
- Her pride is further victimised by being forced into the role of both parents.

Debatable from several angles...but with the learned behaviors that life brings as well as the buoyance of truth to re-surface; many of the ills that still plague us is due to our own adherence and arrogance to recognition. Aside from TRUTHFUL personal preferences this relationship has been destroyed. One aspect is by destroying the Blackman's economic power, which further effects his ability to be viewed by his woman as a man...the demotion of the black-man with the promotion of the black-woman has been the catalyst that caused many woman to ignore the intentional subjugation of their counterparts who were incurring the other hand of discord by the same benefactor. The mechanisms and politics are measurable, but the results are enormous. Again, I re-iterate the ideals of roles in society flipped on its head in this case...and with no religious fortification to further instill discipline, the case is lost before it ever comes before adjudication. The broken family and offspring by unwed & unwanted pregnancy brews more resentment from trivial animosities proportionalized by underlying pressures that have pinned a nation of people against one another. The house Negros vs field nigger, and love towards the master for what little he shares that establish hierarchical statuses among the same people...It's a bit harsh, but true...and we all need to deal with these issues head on and not is some sugar-coated method of political correct bull crapt that leaves things open ended after a few disagreeances. Anger has overtaken the ability of dialogue, and frustration has reinforced violence.

Young girls are taught early by often neglectful fathers, who now don't want the same things to occur to their own daughters; while sons' are advised about the fast actions of teenage girls looking to latch onto meal tickets from poverty level existence grouping athletes etc. show casing feminine assets as bait. It's a dark and gloomy cycle that has spiraled downward into a very murky & limited existence.

Some of the other points already made earlier as to the overall battle between the sexes as we see now more so today in the west come to mind. The conditions of life/ survival supersede the fundamental reasoning that lies at the base of the designed conditions and therefore nothing of meek regards are offered, only the rashness of this material world in efforts to stay afloat desired wishes. So, the equilibrium has forever been destroyed although current demand is more than supply making the price for true companionship very expensive. Black women confront the worst relationship market of any group because of economic and cultural forces that are not of their own making...More than two million men are now imprisoned in the U.S., and roughly 40% of them are African-American. At any given time, more than 10% of black men in their 20s or 30s—prime marrying ages—are in jail or prison. But another poll suggests that at every income level, black men are less likely to marry than are their white counterparts. And the marriage gap is wider among men who earn more than $100,000 a year than among men who earn, say, $50,000 or $60,000 a year. Whether I believe that or not, but in terms of the main persuasions of today affecting black men I do see some truth to it, not to mention those of celebrity dating more exotic type of women inaccessible otherwise. But these conditions the many which derive from politics, while the just acceptance of bad personal choices always seems to bring to the conversation between black men and women unlike any other group...is situation of limiting themselves to black men. Another startling conclusion: was Black women can best promote black marriage by opening themselves to relationships with men of other races...No matter what contemporary magazine you read, you want read about such comments being made about other ethnic women; thus re-enforcing my premise to the value of black women.

One thing is for sure, the white man has always had a fondness for the black woman through is curiosity turned rape in the past to his modern realisation of easy pleasing of black woman with his monetary means...Another rare notion that I feel compelled to mention this hate turned love relationship of the victimized black woman toward her captive lover and now political suitor who has turned her head again to the privileges he has to offer in contrast to those withheld from her counterpart. It's quite an ironic situation that has seemed to leap frog decades into the still current affairs of a relationship first destroyed hundreds of years ago.

It's a pretty big deal, and no one reading this should think otherwise...Why? Well, that's because the other groups know the value of their women in carrying on the racial identity of that group and therefore other groups protect and place high moral values over there women, while the black-women is under classed. I believe love is blind and therefore don't frown upon interracial marriages, however I do frown upon cohersed conditions that were originally not there to begin with. Could it be that the black identity itself is under attack? Well, it surely leads one to think so with today's police policies. Whether its openly disclosed as true fact or not, somethings just don't need to said in order to pick up on the motives behind such antics. Not that anything would ever be openly shared by any creditable leadership other than by mistakes, or by opposing racial groups that would be heard but not given any credit towards funding, promoting, or ordering such cases on a national or international level.

One such recent conspiracy theory

In the light of recent motives and the explosion of Black Death at the hand of police, is the conspiracy to kill blacks for their organs...2013 these two extreme cases surfaced.

- 17 year old Kendrick Johnson of Georgia was found inside of a rolled up mat at Lowndes High School. Johnson's body was upside down inside of the mat which had been placed upright behind bleachers. His internal organs were missing and the cavities were filled with newspaper. His death was ruled an accident.

- 24 year old Ryan Singleton of Atlanta made news just last week. His body was discovered in the desert of Death Valley by joggers. All of his organs were missing. These two stories have led to a conspiracy theory that there is a black market for black organs.

Dick Gregory said in an interview, **"The undertaker that dealt with Kendrick Johnson is the same undertaker from Miami that was used to deal with Trayvon Martin.** You mean to tell me as close as Atlanta is, you're going to call a black undertaker way from Florida?" Gregory said he always felt there was something fishy about the Trayvon Martin case. "When have you seen a homicide with an emphasis on what was purchased? That's because he never went to that store." He believes Martin's organs were harvested. "The biggest money maker in the country is organs," he said. What they get paid: $600 for a brain, as much as $850 for an elbow, up to $850 for a hand, according to an analysis of market prices for fresh or frozen body parts used for research and education that was conducted by Annie Cheney, author of *Body Brokers: Inside America's Underground Trade in Human Remains*. **Henrietta Lacks** as was an African American woman who went to Johns Hopkins Hospital in 1951 because of a painful knot in her stomach and abnormal bleeding after giving birth to her fifth child. She was diagnosed with cancer and two parts of her cervix were removed (the healthy part and the cancerous part) without her permission. The doctors discovered that Lacks cells kept alive and grew. **Her** cells were named HeLa and for over six decades, they have been used more 74,000 **studies.** As a result HeLa were the first human cells to be successfully cloned. Not so far-fetched when you consider these above facts documented in police and or medical records with all the suspicious annotations attached to them. Even, today upon entrance into the USA penial system DNA is harvested from each subject by drawing blood. This isn't a choice, as the state believes they are entitled to everything but your soul which, is only free by their inability to physically jail it. Taken on the premise that such DNA would be used to identify convicted felons; I guarantee its acquisition is also used in research. http://www.theafrolounge.com/2013/10/30/conspiracy-theory-black-people-being-murdered-for-their-organs/. In 2006, the USA Today wrote an investigative report that was prompted by more than 16,000 outstanding lawsuits of families all claiming to have had loved ones missing body parts.

In January of 2015, the FBI raided a Chicago operation linked to Detroit body parts business http://melanoidnation.org/feds-raid-chicago-operation-linked-to-detroit-body-parts-business/. Truth of the matter is there are many, many cases that go beyond the wishful or imaginary thoughts of erroneous skepticism made conspiracy truth...One characteristic about human beings is our ability to so easily forget, and then after a few small societal adjustments, history is abhorred and forgotten. One such reality is The **Tuskegee syphilis experiment** was an infamous clinical study conducted between 1932 and 1972 by the U.S. Public Health Service to study the natural progression of untreated syphilis in rural African-American men in Alabama. They were told that they were receiving free health care from the U.S. government. The 40-year study was controversial for reasons related to ethical standards, primarily because researchers knowingly failed to treat patients appropriately after the 1940s validation of penicillin as an effective cure for the disease they were studying. 600 impoverished sharecroppers from Macon County, Alabama; 399 had previously contracted syphilis before the study began, and 201 did not have the disease. The men were given free medical care, meals, and free burial insurance for participating in the study. None of the men infected were ever given the cure of penicillin even after it was decided to be the cure. The Tuskegee Syphilis Study, cited as "arguably the most infamous biomedical research study in U.S. history", led to the 1979 Belmont Report and the establishment of the Office for Human Research Protections (OHRP)...As with other laws that have come to protect the rights of people, loop holes and other means are sought to bypass them. The penial system is again the perfect example. Why

should convicts be treated as subjects not granted civil nor the rights over their own bodies besides the term of incarceration they are indebted? Imprisonment should not negate human or civil rights.
(https://en.wikipedia.org/wiki/Tuskegee_syphilis_experiment). Furthermore, the history of bad medical/research against black people, history brings validating evidences. If nothing else it proves that a government has & does carry out malice practices and thereby should never be thought to be underneath any ability of evil. In fact, it would be fair to cite that the entire history of America has been violent, and the violence has been carried relentlessly into her future. It's incomprehensible that people have managed to largely ignore all the violence and live within its shadow with thoughts and ideals that have never been further from the truth.

Going back to the earlier comparisons of today's Palestinian occupation and apartheid oppression; the family unit and unity of the community is as they know too well important to withstand the brutal violence of the Israeli government. Children are born into wed families, and reared usually by two-parent families and the roles of men and woman are followed without the chauvinistic machismo for the orderly fashion of families and society to work. Even under oppressed conditions, it's important to stay guided aright, to one day overcome. One miracle worth mention is that the Creator has made it that 8 out of 10 babies born in the area of Palestine are male. Big deal...yes it is and it's an indication that through subjected suffering persevered with patience and adherence to what is right; the Palestinian people are being raised amongst all people to a position of favor and enabled with male children to continue to fight. Faith and remembrance of the Creator are held and increase even in the difficulty they have faced...their conditions politically are more so a condition of the entire region and its fragmented loyalties toward each other much like that of black Americans today. Nationalism in this regard is the culprit, where self-hatred is for the later... Nonetheless the parallels are there, and lessons can be drawn from both sides. Additionally, the rest of the world should see that freedom is a personal perception that is dynamic and case specific with tailored politics to suit desired outcomes.

Desensitized, conditioned and experimental subjects the changes have been implemented with harshness and randomly adjusted subtly to be maintained. The subtlety of change also goes basically unnoticed right under the noses of the so called "free". Over time the surprise of just how far things have shifted is inconceivable but nonetheless detestable.

Required Action

My new found passion of reality illustration through words has been something I have pondered in the past when troubled by life, adviced to open up through a journal type release of inner feelings and emotions as a sort of self-confession. I took the time to do so initially, but my life was too busy for me to sustain it...my first writings were more or less a chronological order of life experiences and or events that have impacted my life the most. As I continued with the most recent experiences & events, primarily dealing with the death of my mother, I saw the cinematic outline of my life...I was then in my late 20's, but had already accomplished so much and still more was to come. Within my own story, I saw the evolutionary changes I had under gown and why. Many people, never seen this side of my personality, which was in essence the bulk of who I am...I have always since very young had the desire of knowledge, meta-physical, deeper understanding type personality. Simple answers without logic were never satisfying for me; therefore I could never blindly follow anything. Instead; the question would just lie filed away until triggered back to memory with conclusions triggered by conversations, experience, or learned type lectures that would satisfy those unanswered phenomenon. This being the case, it was always applicable to everything I was experiencing. Without praising myself to much or seeking it from you; I honestly can say that I have always seen the world for what it really was and continues to be...

My parents, during the times of our best family years, when there was a slight struggle which made the family bond; I remember sitting with my parents at the kitchen table watching them discuss the bills, and budget of the household. These factions taught me a lot, and also helped me to becoming responsible earlier in life. Growing up on the cusp of Ethnic group, National and

International change, and understanding it is huge to the continuation into that change. The rules were changing to a modified version of an old game so being present to learn the new rules was extremely beneficial. For example, the Qur'an has within it revelations that came as answers or guidance towards events that were unfolding involving the Prophet s.a.w, his companions, and even towards enemies...those who were there to witness the events and then see the corresponding revelation that came as a result or a pre-hindrance to otherwise destined action, have a level of understanding none before them nor after them will ever obtain.

Our most enlightened activist will have been those with first-hand knowledge & experience to offer insight into guidance towards the future. We are again upon another cusp 50yrs later...Unfortunately, we don't seem to have the same political awareness's we had carried over from the era of the 1960's and thus we are finding the world as a whole victimized from exploited duping of masses of people easily divided through difference and sustained with fear. Changes no longer require the time of generational change over's; instead now they happen in an instant and then very easily beamed around the world, articulated and manipulated to brain-washing an un-educated population by denial of truth, and perpetuated lies heard over-n-over again until believed as truth. Thus introverted upon the true nature of our own intellect; reason, logic, and investigation into the truth are now longer needed...rather a heavy rotation cycle in the media is good enough.

I have been fortunate to travel the world, and in doing so it has raised my eyebrow many times to understanding the whole. What I mean, is unlike many less fortunate or seizing opportunistic people, they don't have any concept outside their nationalistic viewpoints and they are more easily controllable because they have lost the connection to the rest of the human family. This thwarted type of racism applied to nationalistic, not visible without police or military checkpoints, is a type of perpetuated divide and keep conquered strategy. This ignorance is often applied towards people of the same ethnicity, & language where there are absolutely NO differences other than Nation of origin or residence. This is ridiculous when one really looks into the idea, and in addition to this division, these boundaries are design to keep people in while others are kept out...Resources are claimed both those in the earth as well as the human capital that we have come to understand the modern enslavement of mankind today through debt. The web of prejudicial entanglement mired in the rhetoric of political motivations today, has become the adhered to speech of those who blindly follow, and willfully accept. But, what's to become of those who don't? Speaking now to those who are inclined to becoming more active, we have a responsibility not only towards ourselves, our children but also unfortunately towards the ignorant who willfully follow the wrong way. Shepherds of humanity, if you will; we have to persuade through convincing the ignorant they are wrong, not conviction through speech...Action is the only way to show people and win them. This is where many of us are today, thinking we can learn a few things, quote a few facts, and instantly win over those whom we are addressing. Well, if you haven't already seen so, you will learn that this is not sustainable nor is it reliable. It may give you temporary results, but the world and all of its tricks can easily undo the simple measure we undergo without actually implementing our words into manifesting and arresting progress towards keeping what is gained. Like two opposing armies, advancements into enemy territory are tactical measures not won by speech alone (politics), but rather by ingenuity of action with knowledge of the others applied notions (tangible action). Today's world and its people are highly materialistic, and therefore the stronger of the two usually is in control of the materialistic gains of the worlds and thereby uses it to but loyalty...this is the first enemy, and the most often under-estimated. Weaker subjects must be shown the sustenance of humble means; otherwise they will very easily abandon everything to return to the manipulation of the material world... "What makes any campaign appropriate or sought as opposed to self-seeking; that it serves the quality of the socio-political order as a whole rather than any particular interest group within it"....Service to one's self and community are the same...So, the same rights, and means we seek individually have to be offered to others otherwise they won't be sustained.

Secondly, many people really just don't care, and that's evident through their actions. I don't stand in judgement of anyone; and I also understand the deception that many of us have fallen victim too. In addition, I understand the other relevant handy-caps of people in becoming victims. However; many of us are today faced with moral questions...modernity and life-styles have enslaved many of us to unbreakable shackles that have enslaved us into systems that perpetuate our own captivity and victimization. Laws of the land and our ignorance toward them keep us defeated and thus inhibit our abilities legally...In-debtedness or dependency is probably the largest group. Modern slaves to paying debt of mortgages and other loans of which many will die before the principals are paid in full, while the dependency of jobs in a busted economy leave many people without the ability to break free. There are some exceptions, but these exceptions are often conditional to ethnicity and thus aren't widely in administered towards a more humanitarian effort.

For example; with no pun intended...I know of groups in Canada, whom are pretty successful in acquiring their neighborhoods' of a fairly new area of homes. Collectively, pooling together the financial strength of each person into a more formidable institution that allows them to escape the interest based banking system, which is a testament to its success and uses. However, what I find wrong with this is although they are able to acquire through a collective purchasing power, they bigger picture is still not addressed or over-looked. Let's face it, many foreign nationals have gone to America and Canada largely for material reasons, not for reasons otherwise told us, be there a few exceptional legitimacies...That being the case education a huge runner up in acquiring the dream, god willing results in successful careers. But those careers are hinged on the back to the overall economy and thus are inclined to dependency. Why is it that these same groups aren't trying to acquire land in the rural areas where instead of seeking six-figure paying careers in the city, those same professions could go toward building the same small villages in the country that are acquired in the city? Think about that...Isn't absolute freedom more rewarding than a six-figure paying career with a currency that is fiat, with no intrinsic value? The building up of the land in the rural area, with farms that produce food and storage facilities initially, then homes, and other businesses...the community would now longer be dependent on the status of the state/provincial economy and thus be self-sufficient and free. Obtaining such a huge advantage would bring about not just victories of those who participate, but could also cater to win others through tangible manifestation of action. This would be the weaker army's advantage in exposing the illusions that glamorously back the material world in exposing the truth to the very definition of sovereign freedoms and thus perhaps display the true desire to help humanity free itself, as oppose to conditional loyalties of materialism...The overall benefit to the human family is the goal; after all what are human beings doing to the contribution of humanity if they are restricted from pursuing their true passions & creativity, and thereby enslaved to carry out others wishes and rewarded with things that will only lead to more self-defeating greed.

The financial withdrawal of the people in systems like America especially is an absolute must...The imperialistic foreign policies of America are coming from your continued participation within her. Yes, as I have already noted, many people are so indebted or dependent that walking away would cause drastic changes; and thus anyone not yet in such a situation should take heed to this very cleverly hidden trap. Working to send money to relatives in other countries many of which, may be in lands in north-Africa or the middle-east isn't something noble in your efforts; because this small effort is undone by your larger contribution to the paid taxes you've earned that aide in bombing those same lands. You have to see the bigger picture and not continue half-awoken...finances fund campaigns, and throughout history you will always see the most powerful where those who had the resources to sustain their agendas. Paper-currency devised by the west and forcibly shared by other countries by elevating it to world reserve currency, has ripped every government off by trading currency for none-back currency that usurps the wealth of sovereign countries (https://www.youtube.com/watch?v=djwPqAJ_3GY). This illusion to participate and consideration of your own well-being at the expense of the majority of the world is the dilemma that the peoples of America and Europe are becoming more so acquainted with today. Their arrogances of seeking hegemony over the rest of the world was troubled from the very foundations of its implementation as nothing that holds the entire world captive is sustainable. In such cases & terms, the few although they may not realize it; are able to make huge ripples in the waves that don't go un-noticed and thus are able to bring about movements of fostering change. But, these ripples have to be rooted in actions, not words...common-minds after self-recognition of purpose have to unite and stand no matter the cause or effect in tireless campaigning for truth and justice. After all, what has the last 50 years been but effective begging of people towards a system of government that ignores its own founding principles and the authority within its citizen's desires and reflective will? That is why differences have always been the #1 bases of exploiting fear & divisions, because without proper unity nothing with be strong enough to withstand the first wave of retaliation, which always will surely be through poverty (otherwise, your individual sustenance). This is why the tangible practice of self-reliance and dependency is so important. Considering history, most recent history i.e. the past 50yrs in terms of civil rights and so forth...and now also taking away the racial element only to the expansion of classism...I see that this common one-sided ignorance, which should be very clear to community leaders as a pacification to true action selling the community short or the true end goal. What I mean by that is, leaders are often paid off by becoming proxies and thus supported in allowing shallow battles to be won, while the disguised notions linger in limbo to carry over into later generations. Any leader, No matter who they are should be people you here calling to the complete and utter destruction of enslavement, and the liberty of collective sovereignty; if he or she does not, then question their motives & or abilities to lead...

So, what do you think? Why aren't we there yet? Can "A" or "The" destination be obtained? The oppression of people...systematically installed and sustained through political policies; then exploited by secular, racial, & cultural divisions. We the people have to again unite under a banner of justice, with open-minded dialogue towards cohesion and upright fairness of all walks of life...Until this happens, maybe the destination is much further off then we think... I leave you with these illustrating words:

thought of evolutionary psychology, perforated impressions of memories captured by a word held in timeless space the essence of the soul outpacing the brain…
consciousness of ourselves charges each exposure positively or negatively to what is obtained…
through relationships shaped by every experience...no longer held in distance of measure the vastness of the abyss as it tires too reach through the 7 heavens…

always trending towards our end with the passage of time & limited by knowledge...of this world thereby contained…
projected outward through infinite channels of expression in sharing our personal messages…
practitioners of man mad systems fall into mechanical thought promised to arrive in the end at seized upon freedoms that should have been present from the start…
"indivisible" human beings not fragmented within themselves are truly individual…
in-harmonious within the self-spawns personal pursuits that paints the image of ones character in immediacy…

caught in the present moment of life's relationship with the whole
placed within it ;holding dominion that was gifted the creation interacts with humanity & with the creator from a position that is service & submissive…
non-corrupted nor partial within itself each organism knows and understands its individuality and responsibility to the collective…
conditioned to conflict, human misery, suffering and endeavor spills over from each one of us into the whole exceeding proportional measures…
successive generations inheritors of the earth don't understand the current crisis and see it as something separate from themselves…
problems of others often become political turmoil's for mankind; issues without a voice looked

down upon or seen through shades of color...
penciled in and erased otherwise unaccounted for in importance & cheated ledgers...
the structure of human nature reproduced and duplicated in mirrored images in vanities not exposed to the dark...
one way glass that no longer penetrates diseased and hardened hearts...
personal competitions of envy & greed drive the momentum of today's regard...
achievements on the back of privilege un-hinge the rights of subjected cases; cities germinate beneath the soil and grow with acid rain... chemically induced foods; the sun replaced by fluorescent lights...
harboring dissatisfaction carrying over from historical ages...
fate of common traits repeated actions to now held folklore & myth of carbon-copied pages...
prophetically foretold disastrous trajectory without changes...
deceitful speech, failed diplomacy and strategic military exchanges...
depressurization of inflated oppression; studying the decisions of common consequences of those who came before us whose footprints have been erased...

"History, mankind, correction, crisis"